The Power of the PATRIOTS

For almost 20 years No. 45509 ran unnamed, but in November 1951 it was given the name
The Derbyshire Yeomanry when it was transferred to Derby from Crewe North. It is seen on 23rd April 1952 fully
coaled at London Road Junction, Derby ready to work an up express.   *J. P. Wilson*

On 10th August 1964, rebuilt 'Patriot' No. 45527 *Southport* leaves Carlisle with the 8.15 am parcels for Crewe. *John Whiteley*

As part of our ongoing market research, we are always pleased to receive comments about our books, suggestions for new titles, or requests for catalogues. Please write to: The Editorial Director, Oxford Publishing Co., Sparkford, Near Yeovil, Somerset, BA22 7JJ.

The Power of the
PATRIOTS

J.S. Whiteley & G.W. Morrison

OPC

Oxford Publishing Co.

No. 45522 *Prestatyn* was the last of the 18 'Patriots' to be rebuilt with the Stanier Type 2A taper boiler, appearing early in 1949. On 6th August 1961 it stands in the shed yard at Leeds, Holbeck whilst allocated to Kentish Town.

Gavin Morrison

First published in 1997

ISBN 0 86093 232 X

Oxford Publishing Co. is an imprint of Haynes Publishing, Sparkford, Nr Yeovil, Somerset BA22 7JJ
Tel. 01963 440635 Fax: 01963 440001
Int. tel: +44 1963 440635 Fax: +44 1963 440001
E–mail: sales@jhhaynes.demon.co.uk
Web site: http://www.haynes.com

Printed in Hong Kong

Typeset in Times Roman Medium

Introduction

There will be few people alive today who will be able to remember the 'Patriot' class 4-6-0s in their prime. This was when they carried their fine LMS crimson lake livery and provided the motive power for many of the Midland main line expresses as well as those on the West Coast route, especially the Euston–Birmingham trains. The sight and sound of these handsome locomotives at work would have been a memorable spectacle.

Sadly they were only employed on these top-link duties for a relatively short period during the 1930s as they were rapidly superseded by the Stanier 'Jubilees'. As it happened, the last 'Patriot' to be built, (No. 5551), left Crewe Works in May 1934, only a matter of days before the first 'Jubilee', No. 5552 *Silver Jubilee,* emerged.

The rebuilding, as it was termed by the LMS, of LNWR 'Claughton' class 4-6-0s Nos 5902 *Croxteth* and 5971 *Sir Frank Ree*, has been well documented with different authors detailing what they believed to have been the parts incorporated in the rebuilt locomotives. However, what is agreed by all is that there was in fact very little of the original locomotives used. The main external feature that could be identified was the driving wheel centres, which on these first two 'Patriots', were a larger diameter than on the subsequent members of the class.

No. 5971 was initially put to work with great success on the Settle to Carlisle route and was based at Holbeck depot, Leeds. No. 5902 was used on various duties over the Western Division routes of the LMS. In 1931 trials were conducted between Euston and Manchester with this locomotive against No. 5910, a standard 'Claughton', and No. 5908, a 'Claughton' which was fitted with Caprotti valve gear. These trials consisted of two round trips per locomotive and it was concluded that No. 5902 had performed better on all accounts than the two 'Claughtons'.

Fourteen more 'Patriots' were then constructed at Crewe, between June and the end of October 1931, with a further 35 following during 1933 and 1934, these being built by both Crewe and Derby works. There were only very minor detail differences between the locomotives from the LMS's two workshops.

Trials against the 'Jubilees' were carried out on the Euston–Birmingham expresses in October and November 1934. The conclusion that the 'Patriots' were better steaming locomotives than the taper boiler 'Jubilees' must have caused considerable concern.

Their stay on the Midland Division was short lived, although they were well liked by the crews. A shed allocation list dated September 1935 shows that there was none of the class on this division by that time.

The 'Patriots' were never in the limelight like the 'Royal Scots' and 'Jubilees', so from a very early period they settled down to secondary duties on freight and passenger workings, mainly on the Western Division. Of course, they were frequently called on to deputise for the larger 'Royal Scots', and in the summer months could be seen at the head of 14 coaches or more on additional workings. One of their regular duties was the Manchester–Euston train service via Stoke until the weight restrictions that prohibited the 'Royal Scots' were lifted.

In 1946 a start was made on rebuilding the 'Patriots' with Type 2A Stanier taper boilers, new smokeboxes, double chimneys, new cab and Stanier tenders. In effect the end result was a rebuilt 'Royal Scot', the main external difference being the cab window design. The programme ceased in 1949 with No. 45522 after only 18 had been so treated. These locomotives then spent many years working top link duties and were allocated to Camden, Crewe North, Edge Hill and Carlisle Upperby depots, to name a few.

The appearance of the unrebuilt locomotives altered little over the years, except that No. 45508 was fitted with a stovepipe chimney and

–as can be seen later in this book–completely ruined its appearance! Fortunately, no further examples were so modified.

Generally speaking, in the post war years there were few duties guaranteed to produce a 'Patriot' on a regular basis. They could turn up on nearly anything on the West Coast route, from expresses to humble freights, as well as working across the Pennines from Liverpool to Leeds and along the North Wales coast line.

Routes that saw very little of the unrebuilt examples, and which have therefore proved very difficult to obtain any photographs of, were the Settle and Carlisle line, and north of the border, even though three members of the class did have short spells at Polmadie shed in Glasgow.

If one examines the shed allocations list of the unrebuilt examples over the years it will be seen that they were frequently transferred to a wide variety of Western Division depots. Some of the more notable reallocations away from the WCML sheds were No. 45509 going to Derby in 1951 for seven years, and three to Bristol Barrow Road for working cross country expresses to Birmingham, Leeds and York for a four-year period. No. 45517 went to the former Lancashire & Yorkshire Railway shed of Bank Hall and was frequently seen across the Pennines on the Calder Valley route as depicted in this album.

The introduction to the Western Division of the English Electric Type 4 diesels (later Class 40) from the middle of 1959 soon caught up with the unrebuilt locomotives. No. 45502 was the first to be withdrawn in September 1960. Their duties rapidly became less and less important and in 1961 and 1962 a number of depots, such as Nuneaton, had far more 'Patriots' than they knew what to do with. The type had one final fling on passenger services in the 1960s when they worked the Leeds–Lancaster–Morecambe trains which also saw the last workings of Midland Compounds and 'Crab' 2-6-0s. Nos 45543 and 45550 were the last of the original condition locomotives to be condemned, being withdrawn from Carnforth in November and December 1962 respecitvely.

Although banned from working south of Crewe due to electrification, the rebuilt examples soldiered on, mainly on freights between Crewe and Carlisle, with occasional outings on football specials and workings to North Wales, as well as covering for failed diesels. The end came in December 1965 when No. 45530 *Sir Frank Ree* was withdrawn from Carlisle Kingmoor shed.

As is always the case with our books in the 'Power' series, both John Whiteley and myself wish to express our sincere thanks to all the photographers who have allowed us to use their pictures. We have tried to cover as wide an area as possible where the locomotives were to be seen over the years, and to show every member of the class. This proved to be no easy task and we hope that readers enjoy the end product which has taken several years to complete.

Regrettably, the unrebuilt examples disappeared before the preservation movement had really got going. This was particularly unfortunate as the last two examples were apparently in good condition when withdrawn. In fact, in the end none of the 52 'Patriots' was saved but as we have now entered the age of building steam locomotives again perhaps we might yet see a new one emerge at some time in the future? Of the many types that have been lost in the past, an unrebuilt 'Patriot' would certainly be at or very near the top of my list of locomotives that should be recreated, as they must have been one of the most handsome 4-6-0s to run in this country that have not been preserved.

Gavin Morrison,
Mirfield,
West Yorkshire
1997

The 5XP (later 6P and 7P) 'Patriot' class 4-6-0s

BR No	First LMS No.	Name (Date of naming if not from new)	Date Built	Works No.	Date Re-built	Withdrawn
45500	5971	Croxteth Patriot (1937)	11/30		–	3/61
45501	5902	Sir Frank Ree St Dunstan's (1937)	11/30		–	8/61
45502	5959	Royal Naval Division (1937)	6/32	56	–	9/60
45503	5985	The Leicestershire Regiment (1938) The Royal Leicestershire Regiment (1948)	7/32	57	–	8/61
45504	5987	Royal Signals (1937)	7/32	58	–	3/62
45505	5949	The Royal Army Ordnance Corps (1947)	7/32	59	–	6/62
45506	5974	The Royal Pioneer Corps (1948)	8/32	60	–	3/62
45507	5936	Royal Tank Corps (1937)	8/32	62	–	10/62
45508	6010		8/32	61	–	11/60
45509	6005	The Derbyshire Yeomanry (1951)	8/32	63	–	8/61
45510	6012		8/32	64	–	6/62
45511	5942	Isle of Man (1938)	8/32	65	–	2/61
45512	5966	Bunsen	9/32	66	7/48	3/65
45513	5958		9/32	67	–	9/62
45514	5983	Holyhead (1938)	9/32	68	3/47	5/61
45515	5992	Caernarvon (1939)	10/32	69	–	6/62
45516	5982	The Bedfordshire and Hertfordshire Regiment (1938)	10/32	70	–	7/61
45517	5952		2/33	96	–	6/62
45518	6006	Bradshaw (1939)	2/33	97	–	10/62
45519	6008	Lady Godiva	2/33	98	–	3/62
45520	5954	Llandudno (1937)	2/33		–	5/62
45521	5933	Rhyl (1937)	3/33		11/46	9/63
45522	5973	Prestatyn (1939)	3/33		1/49	9/64
45523	6026	Bangor (1938)	3/33	99	10/48	1/64
45524	5907	Sir Frederick Harrison Blackpool (1937)	3/33	100	–	9/62
45525	5916	E. Tootal Broadhurst Colwyn Bay (1937)	3/33		8/48	5/63
45526	5963	Morecambe and Heysham (1937)	3/33		2/47	10/64
45527	5944	Southport (1937)	4/33		9/48	12/64
45528	5996	R.E.M.E. (1959)	4/33		8/47	1/63
45529	5926	Sir Herbert Walker K.C.B. (until 1937) Stephenson (1948)	4/33	102	7/47	2/64
45530	6022	Sir Frank Ree (1937)	4/33	101	10/46	12/65
45531	6027	Sir Frederick Harrison (1937)	4/33	103	12/47	10/65
45532	6011	Illustrious	4/33	104	6/48	1/64
45533	5905	Lord Rathmore	4/33		–	9/62
45534	5935	E. Tootal Broadhurst (1937)	4/33		12/48	5/64
45535	5997	Sir Herbert Walker K.C.B. (1937)	5/33		9/48	10/63
45536	6018	Private W. Wood V.C. (1936)	5/33	105	11/48	12/62
45537	6015	Private E. Sykes V.C.	7/33	108	–	6/62
45538	6000	Giggleswick (1938)	7/33	109	–	9/62
45539	5925	E. C. Trench	7/33	110	–	9/61
45540	5901	Sir Robert Turnbull	8/33	111	10/47	4/63
45541	5903	Duke of Sutherland	8/33	112	–	6/62
45542	5542		3/34	153	–	6/62
45543	5543	Home Guard (1940)	3/34	154	–	11/62
45544	5544		3/34	155	–	12/61
45545	5545	Planet (1948)	3/34	156	11/48	5/64
45546	5546	Fleetwood (1938)	3/34	157	–	6/62
45547	5547		4/34	158	–	9/62
45548	5548	Lytham St. Annes (1937)	4/34	159	–	6/62
45549	5549		4/34	160	–	6/62
45550	5550		5/34	161	–	12/62
45551	5551		5/34	162	–	6/62

Notes

The first 42 locomotives originally carried the numbers of the 'Claughton' class locomotives they replaced but were renumbered 5500-5541 in 1934. They incorporated some parts of the locomotives they replaced but Nos 5542-5551 were built entirely new and carried these numbers from the beginning. A total of 52 was built; none survive today.

Nos 5500, 5501, 5520-5522, 5525-5528 and 5533-5535 were built at LMSR Derby Works.
Nos 5502-5519, 5523, 5524, 5529-5532 and 5536-5551 were built at LMSR Crewe Works.

Evolution

In the early days of the LMS, its prestige express passenger locomotives were the handsome four-cylinder 'Claughton' class 4-6-0s which had been designed by Bowen Cooke for the London & North Western Railway, 130 of which were built at Crewe between 1913 and 1921. In 1932 No. 6011 *Illustrious* is seen at Crewe. It was to be withdrawn from service in February 1933, but reappeared in April 1933 having been 'rebuilt' as a 'Patriot', subsequently becoming BR No. 45532 *Illustrious* and being further rebuilt with a Stanier Type 2A boiler in June 1948.

A. C. Cawston/John Whiteley Collection

Unnamed 'Claughton' No. 5933 is seen at Derby in the early 1930s. After the introduction of the 'Royal Scot' 4-6-0s in 1927, the 'Claughtons' were demoted to less important duties and withdrawal of the 'Claughtons' commenced in 1932, with all the unrebuilt ones having gone by the end of 1935. After the introduction of the 'Royal Scots' a number of 'Claughtons' were transferred to the Midland Division and coupled with redundant larger capacity tenders from withdrawn Robinson ROD 2-8-0s, as seen fitted to No. 5933. This engine was withdrawn at the end of 1932 and 'rebuilt' as a 'Patriot' at Derby in 1933, subsequently renumbered as BR No. 45521 after having been rebuilt with a Stanier 2A taper boiler in 1946.

F. G. Carrier

Still resplendent in LMS crimson lake livery, or Midland red as it was often known, 'Claughton' No. 5954 stands at Crewe in 1932, substantially unaltered since it was built in 1917. It was withdrawn in December 1932 but reappeared 'rebuilt' in February 1933, renumbered 5520 in 1934, named *Llandudno* in 1937 and was one of 34 'Patriots' not to be rebuilt with a Stanier 2A boiler.

A. C. Cawston/John Whiteley Collection

Performing a duty for which it was designed, 'Claughton' No. 5903 *Duke of Sutherland* is heading an up Euston express near Tamworth. It was one of the first 'Claughtons' to be built at Crewe, in June 1913. Originally LNWR No. 21 it was named after a director of the LNWR. Withdrawn in April 1933 it reappeared as a 'Patriot' in August 1933 and was the last of the 'Claughtons' to be dealt with in this 'rebuilding' programme. In 1934 it was renumbered 5541 by the LMS, but was not further rebuilt. It was withdrawn in 1962.

F. G. Carrier

In 1928 some of the Bowen Cooke LNWR 'Claughton' 4-6-0s were rebuilt by the LMS with large G9½S boilers in an attempt to improve their performance and reduce ever increasing fuel costs. Initially they were classified 5X. No. 6004 *Princess Louise* is seen as reboilered at Crewe in 1932. The new boiler proved to be an excellent steamer and increased the nominal tractive effort of these rebuilt 'Claughtons' in proportion to the increase in boiler pressure from 175lb/sq in to 200lb/sq in, and the alteration to the piston valves and rings succeeded in reducing coal consumption. Although only 20 'Claughtons' were reboilered in this manner, it was an important first step towards the subsequent development of the three-cylinder 'Patriot' 4-6-0s. No. 6004 survived as the last reboilered 'Claughton' and was not withdrawn until April 1949, but was never given a BR number after Nationalisation.

A. C. Cawston/John Whiteley Collection

The reboilered 'Claughtons' were fitted with smoke deflectors shortly after a 'Royal Scot' 4-6-0 had been involved in an accident caused by drifting smoke obscuring the driver's forward vision. In this photograph of No. 5910 *J. A. Bright* at Crewe, the external resemblance to the 'Patriot' class which was to follow is clearly apparent. No. 5910 was withdrawn in April 1937.

F. G. Carrier

Another picture of reboilered 'Claughton' No. 6004 *Princess Louise*, taken at Crewe in the mid 1930s after the fitting of the later type of smoke deflectors with angled tops which replaced the first type of straight side deflectors. Its shed code, 16 Kentish Town, can be seen on the smoke-box door. It ran unnamed from September 1935 until withdrawn following construction of 'Princess Royal'. Pacific No. 6204 which was also named *Princess Louise*.

F. G. Carrier

Following the success of the 'Royal Scot' 4-6-0s and the improved performance of the reboilered 'Claughtons' Derby worked out a new design of 4-6-0 which was required for a new express passenger locomotive of wider route availability than the 'Royal Scots'. This design was a blend of the enlarged 'Claughton' boiler with the three-cylinder chassis of the 'Royal Scot'. Thus a powerful 4-6-0 was to be produced with a lower axle-loading than the 'Royal Scots', and in November 1930 two of the original 'Claughtons', Nos 5902 and 5971, were withdrawn from service for rebuilding to this new design. The term 'rebuilding' is probably a misnomer as only the large driving wheel centres, the bogies and sundry small items were retained in the two new 5XPs which were initially given the official name 'Three-cylinder Converted Claughtons'. Not surprisingly, however, in view of the fact that they were in essence a sort of small edition 'Royal Scot' they were soon referred to as 'Baby Scots'. After rebuilding, and with a Fowler 3,500 gallon tender without coal rails formerly attached to a compound 4-4-0, but before being fitted with smoke deflectors, No. 5971 is near Bingley with an up express in the early 1930s. Having been named *Croxteth* since 1923, it is seen here running without a nameplate, but was given the name *Patriot* in 1937 from former 'Claughton' No. 5964 which had been the LNWR War Memorial engine. Henceforth the class was officially described as the 'Patriot' class, No. 5971 having been given the first number in the class, No. 5500, in the 1934 LMS renumbering scheme.

W. H. Foster.

On test the two new three-cylinder 5XPs proved superior to the four-cylinder reboilered 'Claughtons' and No. 5971 put in some good performances on the Settle and Carlisle line, being shedded at Leeds. When William Stanier succeeded Sir Henry Fowler as Chief Mechanical Engineer of the LMS in 1932 there was a need for passenger locomotives of wide route availability and before his own new designs had been prepared, authorisation was given for a further 40 'Claughtons' to be rebuilt. Although these 'rebuilds' took the numbers of the former 'Claughtons' from which they were supposedly rebuilt, it is very doubtful if many of them actually had any 'Claughton' parts at all, although on paper, no doubt for accountancy purposes, they were rebuilds, to all intents and purposes they were replacement locomotives. No. 5539 *E. C. Trench* was formerly 'Claughton' No. 5925, and is seen on shed at Camden about 1936 alongside 'Princess Royal' 4-6-2 No. 6211 *Queen Maud*. The classification 5XP, which was given to these 'rebuilds' can be seen on the cabside, the P having been added by the LMS in 1928 to differentiate between freight (F) and passenger (P) types. At the time it was shedded at Aston and can be seen fitted with a crosshead vacuum pump beneath the cylinder. Of these 40 'rebuilds', the first 15 were produced at Crewe in 1932, and in 1933 ten were constructed at Derby with the remainder at Crewe. No. 5539 emerged from Crewe in July 1933

C. R. L. Coles

On 23rd April 1939, No. 5500 *Patriot* is on its home shed at Willesden. Being one of the first two locomotives to be 'rebuilt' from 'Claughtons' the larger driving wheel centres were retained which show up clearly when compared with the picture of No. 5539 above. The fluted coupling rods fitted to the first two can also be seen compared with the plain coupling rod of other members of the class.

J. P. Wilson

Despite being renumbered 45506 after Nationalisation, little else has changed to the appearance of *The Royal Pioneer Corps* since it was 'rebuilt' in 1932. It is seen on 11th September 1955 on shed at Nottingham whilst allocated to Carlisle Kingmoor.

J. P. Wilson

The next radical change to the 'Patriots' occurred in 1946 when the first of 18 of the class of 52 were rebuilt with the superb 2A taper boiler which had been fitted to the converted 'Royal Scots' and the two rebuilt 'Jubilees'. Unlike the earlier supposed 'rebuilds', it is fair to say that these 18 'Patriots' were indeed rebuilds as the frames, cylinders and valve gear were the same, but their appearance was certainly very different to the original Fowler parallel boiler 'Patriots'. Apart from the new boiler, the rebuilt 'Patriots were fitted with a Stanier cab which replaced the original Fowler cab and also received new Stanier tenders. No. 45525 *Colwyn Bay* was rebuilt in August 1948 at which time it received its BR number. It is seen very shortly after rebuilding in early experimental BR lined black livery of LNWR style and as first classified 6P, later to be classified 7P by BR. Surprisingly the rebuilt 'Patriots' were not initially fitted with smoke deflectors, although by this time the converted 'Royal Scots' were, having again encountered problems with drifting exhaust.

Ron White

On 21st May 1961 No. 45535 *Sir Herbert Walker K.C.B.* stands at Farnley Junction shed, Leeds whilst allocated to Edge Hill. By this date AWS equipment has been fitted, the battery box for which can be seen on the running plate in front of the cab. From 1948 onwards the rebuilt 'Patriots' were fitted with curved smoke deflectors, very similar to those fitted to the converted 'Royal Scots'.

Gavin Morrison.

A side view of No. 45534 *E. Tootal Broadhurst* at Llandudno Junction shed on 31st March 1963 clearly shows the new Stanier pattern cab which was fitted to the rebuilt 'Patriots', unlike the converted 'Royal Scots' which retained their original Fowler cabs. The Stanier 4,000 gallon 9 tons coal capacity tender can also be seen clearly in this photograph.

Gavin Morrison

Flanked by English Electric diesels, and with overhead electrification in evidence No. 45526 *Morecambe and Heysham* has only a few months left in service. It is seen at Crewe North shed on 18th April 1964 whilst allocated to Carlisle Upperby, and by now often on secondary workings, before being withdrawn in October 1964. On rebuilding, the sandboxes of the 'Patriots' were lowered beneath the running plate, unlike the 'Royal Scots' which retained them in their original position on top.

Gavin Morrison

No. 45531 *Sir Frederick Harrison* is at Crewe North shed, shortly before being withdrawn from service in October 1965. The final 7P classification can be seen on the cabside above the number together with the diagonal yellow stripe which denoted that the locomotive was prohibited from working south of Crewe under the energised 25kV catenary due to height restrictions.

J. R. Carter

The 52 Locomotives

In 1937 No. 5500 *Patriot* is seen at its home shed of Camden, being prepared for its next duty. The 42 5XPs initially took the numbers of the 'Claughtons' from which they were supposedly rebuilt, but in 1934 they were renumbered 5500-5541 by the LMS and the remaining ten, which were unashamedly newly built during 1934, followed on as Nos 5542-5551. The prototype was given the No. 5500, but it was not until 1937 that the name *Patriot* was bestowed on this locomotive, the class subsequently then being officially described as the 'Patriot' class.

C. R. L. Coles

The nameplate of the 'class leader' seen on 22nd March 1959. Although including the inscription of the original LNWR nameplate carried by No. 1914 (later No. 5964), the new nameplate seen in this photograph had been cast in the standard LMS style.

Gavin Morrison

A three-quarter rear view of No. 45500 *Patriot* taken at Crewe North on 22nd March 1959 whilst it was allocated to Willesden. This shows its Fowler 3,500 gallon tender which had 5½ tons coal capacity. The BR 6P classification can be seen above the number, this having been changed from the LMS power classification of 5XP shortly after Nationalisation at the same time the reboilered 'Patriots' were altered from 6P to 7P.

Gavin Morrison

On 14th July 1936 No. 5501 *Sir Frank Ree* arrives at Manchester, London Road with the 8.30am express from Euston, running at this time with a 5½ ton tender without coal rails from a compound 4-4-0. No. 5501 was renamed *St Dunstan's* in 1937 and was never selected for rebuilding on the grounds of certain non standard features which the first twelve members of the class had.

J. P. Wilson

No. 45501 *St Dunstan's* leaves Crewe in the early 1960s with an up express. This picture clearly shows the large centred driving wheels which the first two 'Patriots' had together with the fluted side rods which were also peculiar to these first two locomotives.

M. Welch

On a murky day in the mid 1930s No. 5502, as yet unnamed, is passing Camden soon after leaving Euston with a Birmingham express.

C. R. L. Coles

No. 45502 *Royal Naval Division* is working hard on the 1 in 131 climb out of Carlisle towards Wreay with the 4.5pm Glasgow–Manchester express on 16th July 1957. These parallel boilered 'Patriots' were withdrawn earlier than the reboilered examples and most of them were cut up at Crewe, sadly before one was purchased for preservation. No. 45502 was the first 'Patriot' to be withdrawn, in September 1960.

R. J. Leslie

No. 45503 *The Royal Leicestershire Regiment* of Crewe North is coupled in front of converted 'Royal Scot' No. 46130 *The West Yorkshire Regiment* of Edge Hill, at Leeds City on 28th December 1957 as they wait to take over a Newcastle–Liverpool express from an LNER Pacific.

Gavin Morrison

In 1959 No. 45503 approaches Manchester Victoria with an express from Blackpool.

J. R. Carter

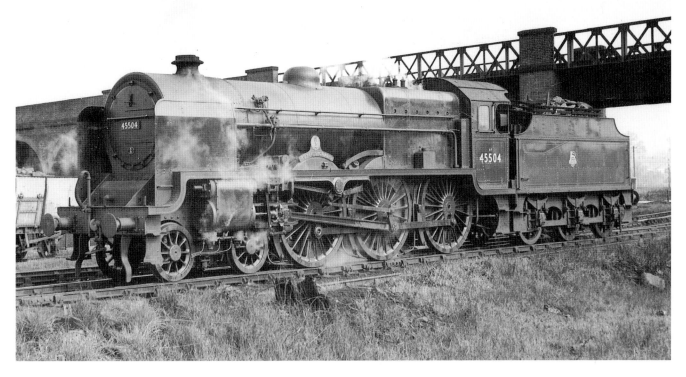

Whilst allocated to Crewe North, No. 45504 *Royal Signals* is seen in commendably clean BR Brunswick green livery at Rugby in the mid 1950s.

J. B. C. McCann

On 23rd August 1960 No. 45504 leaves York with the 12.48pm to Bristol. This was one of three parallel boiler 'Patriots' moved to Bristol Barrow Road in 1958, the other two being Nos 45506 and 45519. All three remained there until withdrawal in March 1962 and whilst working from this depot, by then under Western Region control, they often found their way to Birmingham, Derby and York.

R. J. Leslie

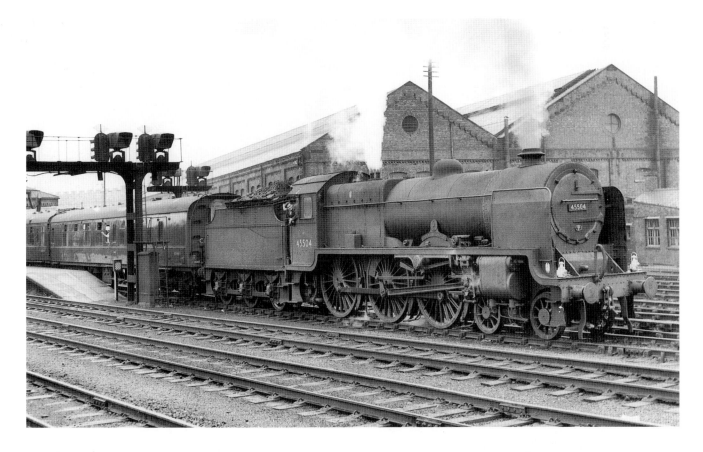

On 12th June 1937 No. 5505 of Camden is seen passing South Kenton with a down express goods. Resplendent in pre-war crimson lake livery, the 'Patriots' were not often seen on goods workings during this period and generally the Camden locomotives were to be seen on Western Division expresses.

A. C. Cawston/John Whiteley Collection

In the early 1960s however, they were often to be seen on goods trains, and on 24th June 1961 No. 45505 *The Royal Army Ordnance Corps* is shown heading south near Hartford with an up express goods. It had been named in 1947 and at that time was allocated to Carlisle Upperby. Here, it is coupled to a straight high-sided, 3,500 gallon tender, No. 4569, with 7 tons coal capacity which was originally paired with a 'Jubilee' 4-6-0, and was one of two which at times were paired with parallel boiler 'Patriots'.

John Whiteley

No. 45506 *The Royal Pioneer Corps* was one of Bristol Barrow Road's trio of 'Patriots'. On 26th July 1960 it leaves Pontefract Baghill with the 8.5am Birmingham–Newcastle which it would have worked as far as York.

P. Cookson

With a full head of steam, No. 45506 departs from Bath Green Park, the most southerly station of the former LMS system, with the Saturday only Bournemouth West–Nottingham on 13th August 1960.

Hugh Ballantyne

On 9th April 1962, in its last year of service, No. 45507 *Royal Tank Corps* has just been coaled at Leeds Holbeck. Having been transferred to Lancaster in February 1962 from Carlisle Upperby, it ended its days working primarily between Morecambe, Lancaster and Leeds before being withdrawn in October 1962.

Gavin Morrison

On Friday, 13th April 1962 No. 45507 is seen shortly after leaving Keighley with a Morecambe–Leeds City train.

Gavin Morrison

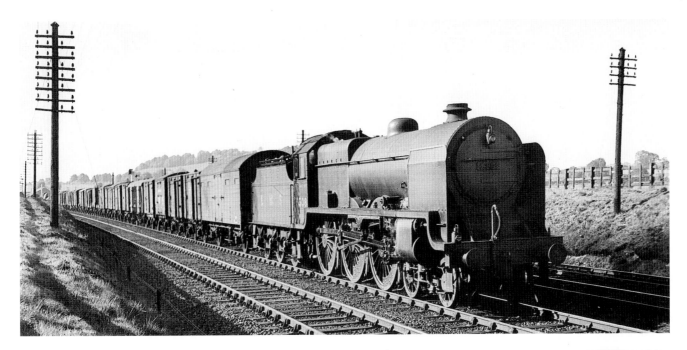

In 1939 No. 5508 of Camden passes Tring with an up express goods. This was one of only ten 'Patriots' never to be given a name, all of which retained their parallel boilers until withdrawal.

C. R. L. Coles

How to disfigure the looks of a supremely handsome locomotive! In 1956 No. 45508 was fitted with an experimental draughting system and this hideous stove-pipe chimney, nicknamed the 'upturned bucket'. Fortunately no further 'Patriots' were so defaced.

Gavin Morrison

Another picture of No. 45508 showing its hideous stove-pipe chimney, taken on 28th June 1957 at Carlisle Upperby, its home shed.

Brian Morrison

From the mid 1930s 'Patriots' were not regular sights on the Midland Division until November 1951 when No. 45509 was named *The Derbyshire Yeomanry* and appropriately transferred to Derby from Crewe North. It remained at Derby for almost seven years during which time it worked on the old Midland main line to St Pancras and also on the York–Bristol route. On 14th June 1954 it is seen at Nottingham Midland on the 1.10pm from Derby.

J. P. Wilson

From Derby No. 45509 was transferred to Newton Heath in August 1958 where it ended its days, being withdrawn in August 1961. On 19th June 1960 it was seen alongside 9F 2-10-0 No. 92161 at Carlisle Kingmoor, clearly displaying its 26A Newton Heath shed plate on the smokebox door. This was one of only six 'Patriots' to be coupled with the same tender for its entire life.

Gavin Morrison

Having been renumbered 5510 in 1934 from its former 'Claughton' number, 6012, it is seen shortly after arrival at Willesden Junction about 1936 with an up express.

C. R. L. Coles

On 9th April 1962, over 25 years later as BR No. 45510, it is at Holbeck depot, Leeds, in substantially the same condition, although rather more grimy.

Gavin Morrison

With only a few weeks in service before being withdrawn, No. 45510 rounds the sharp curve at Shipley, Bingley Junction with a Morecambe–Leeds train, working off Lancaster shed.

Gavin Morrison

Not long after Nationalisation and in dirty external condition No. 45511 *Isle of Man* arrives at Crewe with an up Manchester express.

J. P. Wilson

By the early 1960s the 'Patriots' were often to be seen on freight workings, particularly the unrebuilt engines, and on 9th July 1960 No. 45511 *Isle of Man* has just shut off steam below Shap Summit after a signal check with an up mixed freight.

T. Boustead

On 29th June 1939 No. 5512 *Bunsen* has just arrived at Nottingham Midland with a return Willesden excursion.

J. P. Wilson

Having been fitted with a Stanier 2A taper boiler in July 1948 *Bunsen* is seen at Newton Heath on 7th December 1963. The rebuilt 'Patriots' outlasted the parallel boiler locomotives and this was one of the last to be withdrawn from service, in March 1965. The difference between the Stanier cab which replaced the Fowler version is very apparent in these two photographs.

Gavin Morrison

On a wet 11th March 1961 No. 45513 leaves Carlisle with the 4.10pm to Preston.

R. J. Leslie

Another picture of No. 45513 whilst working from Carnforth sees it climbing away from Carlisle near Wreay with a southbound parcels in the early evening of 15th May 1961.

R. J. Leslie

In the mid 1930s No. 5514 is seen with a backing plate but before being named *Holyhead* in 1938.

Ron White

No. 5514 was reboilered in March 1947 and is seen passing Heaton Norris, nearing Stockport, with a Manchester–Birmingham express in March 1958, carrying its BR number, 45514. At this time it was allocated to Camden and the first style of BR lion and wheel emblem can be seen on the tender. *Holyhead* was the first of the rebuilt 'Patriots' to be withdrawn, in May 1961.

T. Lewis, Norman Preedy Collection

No. 45515 *Caernarvon* of Newton Heath is piloting a 'Black Five' 4-6-0 at York as they prepare to depart with the Heaton–Red Bank empty newspaper vans on 9th August 1961.

P. Cookson

The following day, 10th August 1961, No. 45515 again crossed the Pennines, this time on an easier working, a Manchester–Leeds Central local via Halifax and Bradford. It is passing the site of the long since closed station at Wyke & Norwood Green.

Gavin Morrison

On 24th July 1937 No. 5516 was at Rugby, still unnamed and with tender No. 3187 without coal rails. This tender had originally been attached to an LMS compound 4-4-0 but was fitted to No. 5971 (5500) shortly after it had been 'rebuilt' in 1930, until it was transferred to No. 5516 in February 1935. It remained attached to No. 5516 until February 1952.

This 'Patriot' was fitted with the longest of the names, *The Bedfordshire and Hertfordshire Regiment*, bestowed in 1938, and the large nameplate shows up well in this picture of No. 45516 taken in the early 1960s at Patricroft. The plain side rods fitted to all but the first two of the class can also be seen clearly as can the BR 6P classification on the side of the cab.

J. R. Carter

For several years during the 1950s the Liverpool Exchange–Newcastle train was worked by one of Bank Hall's trio of 'Jubilees', *Mars, Dauntless* or *Glorious,* but in 1958 No. 45517 was transferred there from Willesden and became a regular sight on this train until being withdrawn in June 1962. On 17th February 1960 it has just emerged from Elland Tunnel on this train which it worked as far as York.

Gavin Morrison

On 10th August 1958, whilst it was still on loan to Bank Hall before being permanently allocated there in November 1958, No. 45517 is seen leaving Sowerby Bridge with the 10.30am Liverpool Exchange–Newcastle. It is interesting to note that between the dates these two photographs were taken No. 45517 had been fitted with AWS equipment, the battery box for which can be seen towards the rear of the running plate in the later picture, above.

Gavin Morrison

No. 45518 *Bradshaw* storms out of Leeds past the remains of Holbeck Low Level station with a Leeds City–Morecambe parcels train on 1st May 1962.

Gavin Morrison

An interesting overhead view of *Bradshaw* taken at Crewe showing the cab with open roof ventilator and the front section of the Fowler tender with its coal rails.

M. Welch

Numerically the last of Bristol Barrow Road's trio of parallel boiler 'Patriots', No. 45519 *Lady Godiva*. It is seen leaving Pontefract Baghill on one of its regular trips to York with the 8.5am Birmingham–Newcastle on 18th June 1960.

P. Cookson

No. 45519 passes Chaloner Whin Junction, York on 18th May 1959 on its way back to the South West, working a Newcastle–Bristol express.

Gavin Morrison

Shortly after being 'rebuilt' from a 'Claughton' and still with its former 'Claughton' number, No. 5954, is seen at Derby awaiting its next duty. Resplendent in 'Midland red' livery its classification 5XP is unusually positioned adjacent to the cab window and not above its cabside number, as was the more usual fashion. It was to be renumbered 5520 in September 1934 and named *Llandudno* in 1937.

F. G. Carrier

On 30th August 1949 No. 45520 *Llandudno* awaits departure from Birmingham New Street. This photograph shows its early Nationalisation livery of post-war LMS lined black with the words British Railways applied to the tender before the first BR lion and wheel emblem was in regular use, having been introduced in the spring of 1949.

Norman Preedy Collection

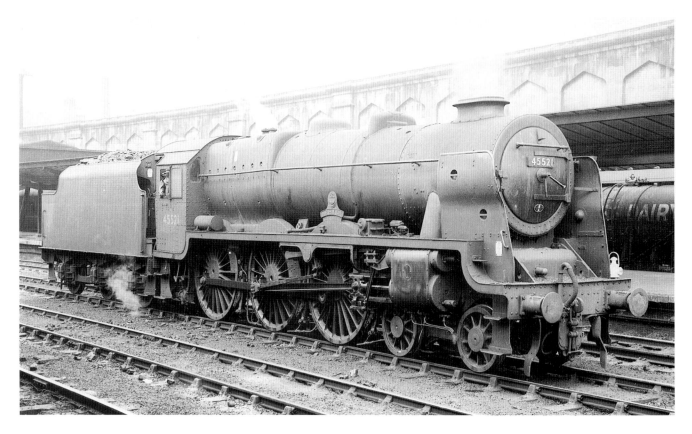

No. 45521 *Rhyl* had been rebuilt with a Crewe 2A taper boiler in 1946 and whilst allocated to Edge Hill stands at Carlisle on 12th August 1961, waiting to take over a southbound express.

Norman Preedy

After Nationalisation No. 45521 spent most of its time at Edge Hill and was no stranger to Trans Pennine workings such as this, the morning Newcastle–Liverpool which it had taken over at Leeds City. It is passing Gledholt on the long climb out of Huddersfield on 18th October 1959.

Gavin Morrison

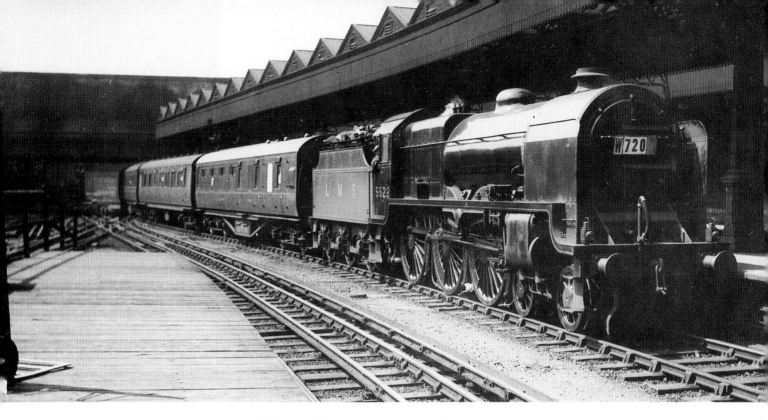

Before being named *Prestatyn* in 1939, No. 5522 arrives at Euston in 1938 with an excursion.

C. R. L. Coles

After rebuilding No. 45522 *Prestatyn* prepares to leave Leeds City with the 12.35pm to St Pancras on 28th August 1961 whilst allocated to Kentish Town.

Gavin Morrison

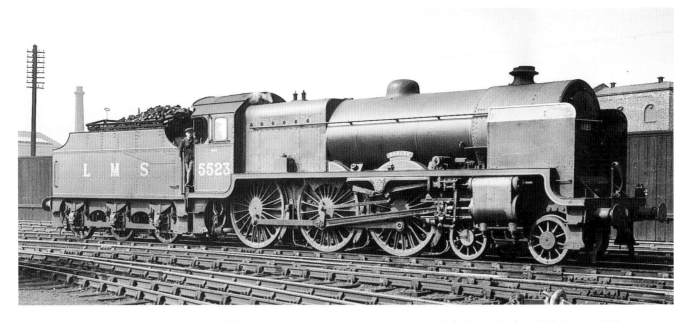

Having been named in 1938, No. 5523 *Bangor* was photographed at Crewe North, its home shed, on 20th August 1939.

J. P. Wilson

In 1959 No. 45523 speeds through Cheddington with an up Blackpool express.

M. Welch

No. 45524 *Blackpool* was named *Sir Frederick Harrison* until 1937 when that name was transferred to No. 5531. It leaves Windermere on 6th July 1960 with the up 'Lakes Express' whilst allocated to Carlisle Upperby.

T. Boustead

No. 45524 rests between duties at Patricroft in 1961 whilst allocated to Edge Hill. The electrification flashes can be seen on the lower part of the smoke deflector denoting that it could be working beneath overhead live wires.

J. R. Carter

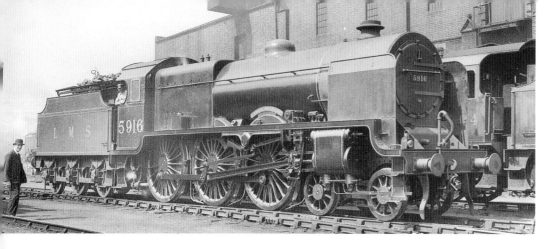

With its former 'Claughton' number 5916, *E. Tootal Broadhurst*, is caught by the camera on shed at Kentish Town, not long after appearing from Derby in 1933.

Ron White

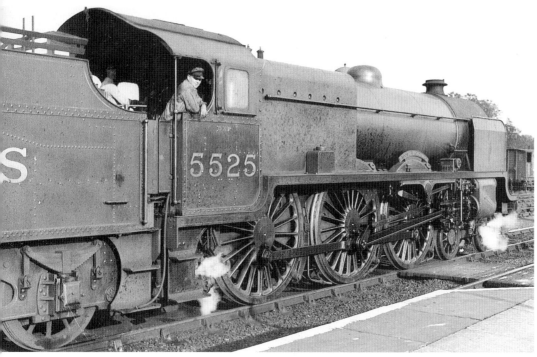

No. 5525 stands at Watford Junction about 1936, having been renumbered from 5916 in 1934, but before being renamed *Colwyn Bay* in 1937. At the time of renumbering the 5XP classification was moved from beside the cab window to underneath.

C. R. L. Coles

In August 1948 *Colwyn Bay* was rebuilt with a 2A taper boiler. Shortly after being rebuilt and before the addition of smoke deflectors, it accelerates an up express away from its Rugby stop whilst allocated to Crewe North.

J. B. C. McCann

No. 45526 *Morecambe and Heysham* was rebuilt in 1947 after which it spent most its working life at Carlisle Upperby until being withdrawn in October 1964. In 1962 it is depicted approaching Monton Green on the Tyldesley–Wigan line with the 7pm Manchester Liverpool Road–Carlisle freight.

J. R. Carter

In sparkling BR Brunswick green livery No. 45526 climbs away from Carlisle, just south of Wreay, on Easter Monday, 3rd April 1961 heading a 15-coach relief Glasgow–Birmingham.

R. J. Leslie

This side view of No. 45527 *Southport* shows the beautifully proportioned lines of the rebuilt 'Patriots'. It is seen at Leeds Holbeck motive power depot after working a football special from Carlisle on Saturday, 21st January 1964.

Gavin Morrison

On 21st December 1963 No. 45527 pauses at Hellifield with a Stourton–Carlisle freight whilst allocated to Carlisle Kingmoor from where it was withdrawn in December 1964.

Gavin Morrison

No. 45528 was rebuilt in August 1947 and is seen before being fitted with smoke deflectors, passing Longsight No. 1 signal box with what appears to be a running in turn to Crewe. With the exception of No. 45528, all the taper-boiler 'Patriots' bore names at the time they were rebuilt, but this locomotive was not named until September 1959, barely three years before it was withdrawn.

T. Lewis

Having been named *R.E.M.E.,* No. 45528 was at Farnley Junction shed, Leeds, on 26th June 1960.

Gavin Morrison

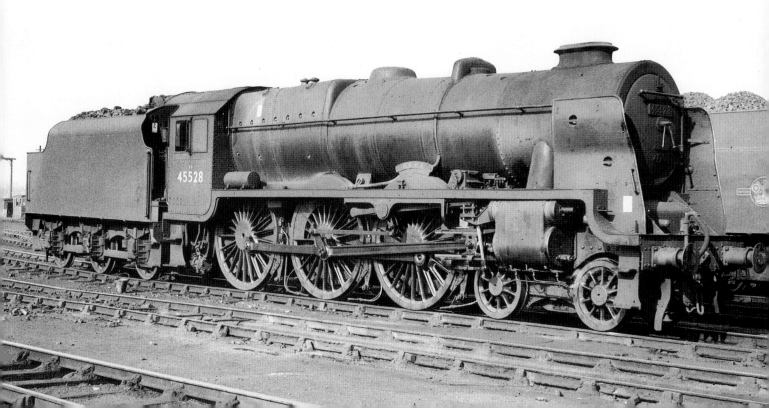

No. 45529 *Stephenson* drifts downhill from Shap Summit in 1960 with an up express.

T. Boustead

Whilst allocated to Willesden, No. 45529 is being turned at Patricroft in 1961. After being rebuilt in 1947 this locomotive was continually transferred between Camden and Crewe North for almost ten years before spending about three years at Willesden from early 1961. It ended up at the former Great Central shed at Annesley towards the end of 1963 from where it was withdrawn in February 1964.

J. R. Carter

No. 45530 *Sir Frank Ree* on shed at Crewe North in 1961 whilst allocated to Willesden. This was the first of the 'Patriots' to be rebuilt with the 2A taper boiler, emerging in October 1946 and classified 6P which was later altered to 7P by BR. Although rebuilt under the regime of H. G. Ivatt after the retirement of Sir William Stanier, the design was obviously Stanier inspired and was very similar to his two rebuilt 'Jubilees' introduced in 1942 and his converted 'Royal Scots' introduced in 1943, all of which incorporated the superb Crewe 2A taper boiler. Eighteen 'Patriots' were eventually rebuilt over a 2½-year period as more class 6P power was required after the Second World War, seemingly in a rather haphazard fashion, although none of the first twelve of the class were rebuilt because of their non-standard features. Although the end of steam was not in sight at this post war period, surprisingly no further rebuilding was authorised and 34 'Patriots' retained their parallel boilers until eventual withdrawal in the 1960s.

M. Welch

Although No. 45530 *Sir Frank Ree* was the first of the 'Patriots' to be rebuilt it was the last to be withdrawn, in December 1965 – three years after No. 45550 which was the last of the unrebuilt 'Patriots' to be withdrawn. Whilst allocated to Longsight it is shown heading an up Manchester express.

T. Lewis

A fine portrait of No. 45531 *Sir Frederick Harrison* which was the last of eight to be rebuilt under the auspices of the LMS, the remaining ten appearing after Nationalisation. It is seen in Derby Loco Works yard on 15th May 1948 newly repainted in experimental light apple green livery with LNWR style red, cream and grey lining. In common with other experimental liveries, this did not wearparticularly well in everyday service and in the spring of 1949 the Railway Executive announced details of its new standard liveries. This was LNWR black, with the exception of top link express passenger classes, which were to be Brunswick green with black and orange lining, this including the 'Patriots'.

J. M. Jarvis

No. 45531 spent most of its time in reboilered form at Edge Hill, and displaying its 8A Edge Hill shedplate it is seen resting between duties at Farnley Junction, Leeds on 9th July 1960. This was the penultimate 'Patriot' to be withdrawn, on 30th October 1965.

Gavin Morrison

No. 5532 *Illustrious* was one of Bushbury's well-maintained 'Patriots' in the pre-war years, often working the Euston–Birmingham two-hour expresses. However, it is seen here working an up Cup Final excursion near Headstone Lane.

C. R. L. Coles

Having been rebuilt in 1948, No. 45532 approaches Chinley North Junction with a Manchester–St Pancras express whilst allocated to Nottingham.

T. Lewis, Norman Preedy Collection

Having been renumbered early in 1949, No. 45533 *Lord Rathmore* is seen at Rugby on 12th August 1949 in post-war lined black livery, with the lettering 'British Railways' on the tender which preceded the large lion over wheel emblem that first appeared in 1949.

J. M. Jarvis

In the summer of 1959 No. 45533 runs in to Crewe with an up Manchester express.

M. Welch

Towards the end of its life No. 45534 *E. Tootal Broadhurst* was a regular performer on the North Wales coast line whilst allocated to Llandudno Junction, and on 31st March 1963 is seen at its home depot.

Gavin Morrison

In very presentable external condition No. 45534 is turned at Patricroft MPD in 1962 whilst allocated to Llandudno Junction. In this picture, the 1956 style of tender emblem can be seen which incorporates a lion standing on a crown in a circle with the words 'British Railways' extended either side. Initially the lion always faced forwards, but from about 1957 it was decreed that it should always face left irrespective of which side of the tender it was on.

J. R. Carter

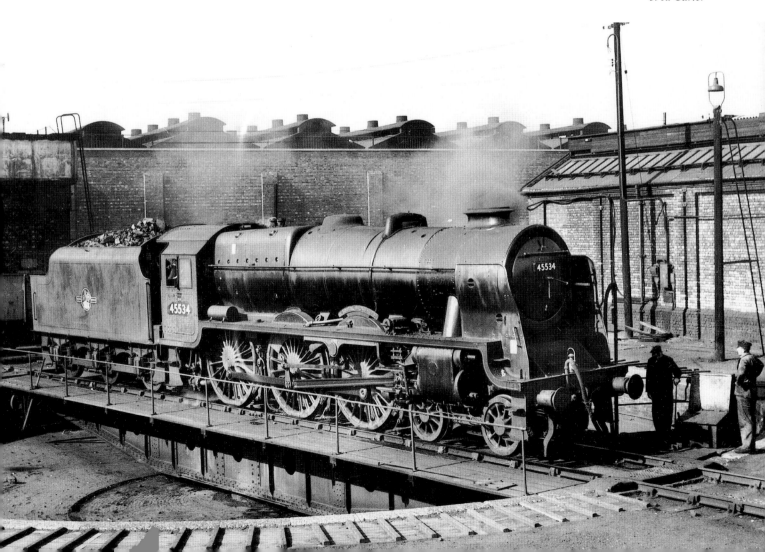

In the summer of 1936 No. 5535 was transferred to Leeds Holbeck and is seen there as fitted with an experimental top feed ahead of the dome on one side only, which it had until mid 1938.

Ron White

In 1935 No. 5535, as yet unnamed, poses at Camden, still fitted with crosshead vacuum pump.

A. C. Cawston/John Whiteley Collection

No. 5535 was named *Sir Herbert Walker K.C.B.* in 1937 and was rebuilt in 1948, seen here as No. 45535 on 11th May 1963 on shed at Perth having worked in from Carlisle.

Gavin Morrison

Whilst allocated to Millhouses, No. 45536 *Private W. Wood V.C.* is seen at Leeds City awaiting the arrival of the up 'Devonian' from Bradford Forster Square which it will take on its journey south.

J. R. Carter

On 23rd March 1961 No. 45536 was on shed at Leeds Holbeck displaying its 41C Millhouses shed code on its smokebox door.

Gavin Morrison

No. 45537 *Private E. Sykes V.C.* ended its days allocated to Nuneaton where it was used on a variety of secondary workings. It is shown standing at Rugby depot in 1960 in front of a Class 3F 0-6-0.

Norman Preedy

This low angle view of No. 45537, taken at Patricroft in 1960, shows the AWS fitted.

J. R. Carter

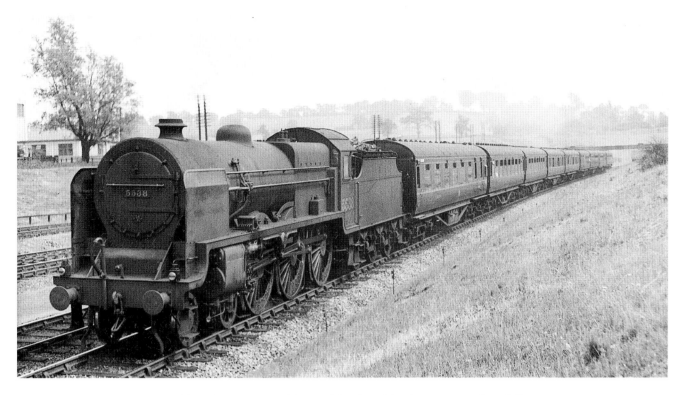

In 1938 No. 5538, named later that year, passes Elstree with a down Manchester express from St Pancras.

C. R. L. Coles

Over 20 years later this unrebuilt 'Patriot' is still in essentially the same condition, but it is now No. 45538 *Giggleswick*. On 25th July 1959 it is seen just south of Tamworth heading an up goods train.

T. Boustead

Edge Hill's No. 45539 *E. C. Trench* waits to leave Liverpool Lime Street on an up train in the late 1950s.

John Whiteley Collection

In August 1961 No. 45539 approaches Deal Street signal box near Manchester Exchange station with an eastbound goods train to Miles Platting.

J. R. Carter

In experimental light apple green livery and before the addition of smoke deflectors, No. 45540 *Sir Robert Turnbull* leaves Rugby with an up express.

J. B. C. McCann

No. 45540 passes Cheadle Hulme with the up 'Comet' from Manchester London Road on 22nd August 1959 as work progresses on the overhead electrification.

T. Lewis, Norman Preedy Collection

Whilst allocated to Longsight, No 5541 *Duke of Sutherland* passes South Kenton in 1938, with a Euston–Manchester express. Although the tender does not appear to be very clean, what a fine sight this pre-war LMS train makes with the locomotive and rolling stock all in matching crimson lake livery and carriage destination boards white with black lettering.

A. C. Cawston/John Whiteley Collection

A 15-coach Glasgow–Liverpool is nearing Thrimby Grange on the southbound climb to Shap Summit behind No. 45541 *Duke of Sutherland* and 'Jubilee' 4-6-0 No. 45706 *Express*.

R. J. Leslie

No. 45542 was the first of the last ten 'Patriots' which were all built at Crewe in 1934 and classed as new engines, unlike the earlier engines which were officially regarded as being rebuilt from 'Claughtons'. In 1949 it was found on shed having been renumbered by BR but with no crest or lettering on its tender and with the 5XP classification on the cabside beneath its number.
Ron White

Heading an up express No. 45542 passes engineering work just north of Crewe. On the left is the original Plasser tamping machine.

M. Welch

Shortly after being transferred to Carnforth, from where it was withdrawn later the same year, No. 45543 *Home Guard* is near Whitehall Junction as it leaves Leeds on 6th June 1962 heading the 1.54pm to Carnforth.

Gavin Morrison

Also whilst shedded at Carnforth, No. 45543 is seen on the turntable at Patricroft with not long to go before withdrawal in November 1962 as the penultimate unrebuilt 'Patriot'.

J. R. Carter

No. 45544 was one of six of the batch of ten new 'Patriots' built in 1934 at Crewe never to be given a name. On 1st April 1961 it passes Winwick Junction, north of Warrington, with a freight coming off the Earlestown line.

Hugh Ballantyne

On 21st October 1952 No. 45544 pilots a Stanier 'Black Five' 4-6-0 away from Birmingham New Street on a Liverpool train.

Norman Preedy Collection

Nicely turned out No. 5545 of Longsight is on shed at Bletchley on 29th May 1937, still fitted with a crosshead vacuum pump.

J. M. Jarvis

No. 45545 was the only one of the last ten 'Patriots' to be rebuilt with a Crewe 2A taper boiler, in November 1948, at which time it was named *Planet*. In 1949, whilst allocated to Camden and before being fitted with smoke deflectors, it is seen leaving Rugby with an up express.

J. B. C. McCann

In its final state No. 45545 rests between duties at Leeds Holbeck on 5th February 1964, shortly before being withdrawn.

Gavin Morrison

On 22nd March 1949 No. 45546 *Fleetwood* posed for the photographer at Rugby shed, still classified 5XP and with 'British Railways' lettered on the tender.

J. M. Jarvis

With the large BR lion and wheel emblem on its tender and now classified 6P No. 45546 awaits departure from Euston in the mid 1950s.

M. Welch

A rather grimy No. 5547 passes Tring with a Euston–Liverpool express in the early post-war years whilst allocated to Edge Hill.   *C. R. L. Coles*

In 1960 No. 45547 is ready for its next turn at Patricroft motive power depot.   *J. R. Carter*

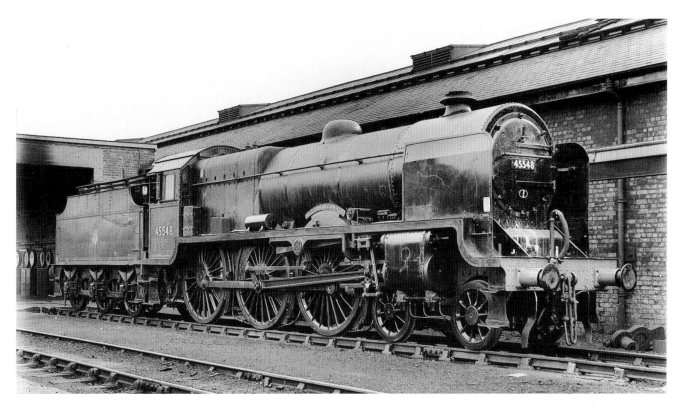

On 2nd October 1960 No. 45548 *Lytham St. Annes* is seen just ex works at Crewe. Numerically this was the last of the 'Patriots' to carry a name and was one of 13 to be named after holiday resorts in the North of England and North Wales served by the LMS, including the Isle of Man which was reached by ferry.

Hugh Ballantyne

Heading an up express in 1959, No. 45548 speeds past Leighton Buzzard.

M. Welch

Seen from a passing train, No. 45549 is at the north end of Tring Cutting heading an up freight.

M. Welch

In 1954 No. 45549 climbs towards Grayrigg near Lambrigg crossing, heading a Crewe–Carlisle parcels whilst allocated to Carlisle Kingmoor.

W. H. Foster

No. 45550 is at Springs Branch, Wigan, on 4th April 1953 attached to the straight high-sided 3,500 gallon tender which it had from 1942 until 1956. In 1943 names were selected for seven 'Patriots' which at that time were not named, but none of these was ever carried. No. 5550 was to have been named *Sir Henry Fowler*, but this locomotive was one of ten members of the class which ran unnamed for their entire existence.

Ron White

On Wednesday, 16th May 1962 No. 45550 is shown near Marley Junction, Keighley, heading the 5.10pm Bradford Forster Square–Morecambe train. Having been built in 1934, it was the last of the unrebuilt 'Patriots' to be withdrawn from service, in December 1962, substantially unaltered for almost 30 years. Sadly all these elegant parallel boiler locomotives were cut up quickly before one could be secured for posterity by the preservation movement.

Gavin Morrison

No. 45551 is seen on shed in commendably clean condition on 25th May 1952.

Ron White

In 1958 No. 45551 was paired with one of the straight high-sided 3,500 gallon tenders until withdrawal in June 1962. Photographed at Carlisle Upperby on 10th September 1959 it awaited a visit to the works.

Gavin Morrison

The LNWR Main Line South of Crewe

Apart from an eight-month spell at Bushbury between 1st October 1949 and 10th June 1950, No. 45536 *Private W. Wood, V.C.* is recorded as being allocated to Longsight after being reboilered for most of its career until withdrawal on 29th December 1962, when it had covered an estimated 1,638,862 miles. At the height of its career it is seen at the buffer stops of Platform No. 2 at Euston, having worked the up 'Mancunian', the clock indicating 1.29pm. The character on the track at the side of the locomotive looks as if he has a hammer in his left hand, and is about to carry out a wheel tapping inspection of the stock.

M. Welch

What a superb sight No. 5533 *Lord Rathmore* makes in its immaculate LMS red livery as it simmers gently at the buffer stops of No. 2 platform at Euston after working an up Birmingham express. It had a 3½-year spell at Bushbury between September 1935 and March 1939, prior to which it had been at Kentish Town. After that it moved around the West Coast Main Line sheds, eventually finishing its days at Edge Hill on 15th September 1962 with a total of 1,311,657 miles covered.

J. G. Dewing

In the early evening on a summer's day in the late 1950s, No. 45538 *Giggleswick* starts an express from Euston and prepares for its assault of Camden Bank.

M. Welch

Prior to being named *Home Guard* in 1940, No. 5543 is shown on the down 'Mancunian' at the top of Camden Bank, one mile out of Euston, on 19th July 1939. It was allocated to Longsight between 12th March 1938 and 19th September 1939, and no doubt worked this train regularly. It had previously been at the depot for 4½ years between 1935 and 1939. It finished its career allocated to Carnforth from 2nd June 1962, not long after a visit to Crewe Works. It appeared on trains over the Midland line to Leeds, but was eventually placed in store at Preston, where it was damaged by a fire at the depot. It was withdrawn on 17th November 1962, having totalled 1,331,749 miles.

J. P. Wilson

During its period of allocation to Willesden between 13th June 1953 and 26th July 1958, No. 45517 was normally employed on express freight duties. Here it is shown at Wembley Central in May 1958 on a down express freight, two months later it moved to Bank Hall, primarily for working the 10.30am Liverpool Exchange–Newcastle express via the Calder Valley main line. It was withdrawn from Bank Hall on 9th June 1962 with 1,328,802 miles credited to it.

C. R. L. Coles

At the peak of its career, when it was sharing duties with the LMS Pacifics on duties such as the 'Merseyside Express', No. 45531 *Sir Frederick Harrison* is seen at the head of 'blood and custard' stock as it passes Kenton alongside the electrified Bakerloo Line of the London Underground system in July 1954. Looking extremely well turned out by Edge Hill, which was its home base for over 13 years between 1950 and 1963, it was also a frequent performer on the Trans Pennine expresses between Liverpool Lime Street and Leeds. It finished its career at Springs Branch, Wigan on 30th October 1965, having covered 1,719,588 miles.

C. R. L. Coles

No. 45503 *The Royal Leicestershire Regiment* thunders north past Headstone Lane against a stormy sky on a Euston–Colne special working on 30th July 1954. The 5A shed code shows it was at Crewe North at the time. Withdrawal came on 12th August 1961 when it was at Upperby after it had covered 1,265,281 miles. Again, the Bakerloo Line can be seen on the right of the picture.

C. R. L. Coles

No. 45510 passes Headstone Lane with a down express freight in April 1957. It was a Willesden locomotive between January 1955 and October 1959. Withdrawal came on 9th June 1962 when at Lancaster, having covered 1,336,022 miles.

C. R. L. Coles

The gangers are standing far enough back, as is the photographer, to avoid being soaked as No. 45534 *E. Tootal Broadhurst* overflows its tender on Bushey Troughs on a down Euston–Liverpool express in August 1956. It was a regular performer on these duties whilst allocated to Edge Hill between November 1951 and November 1959, after which it went to Llandudno Junction for a short spell.

C. R. L. Coles

This view of Bushey, 16 miles from Euston, shows No. 45547 approaching the water troughs with an up twelve-coach express. Bushey station can be seen in the distance beyond the rear of the train.

M. Welch

A superb study of No. 45507 *Royal Tank Corps* passing over Bushey Troughs with a Manchester–South Coast express, which would travel via the North London line with a locomotive change around Willesden. The photograph was taken in August 1954 when it was allocated to Crewe North, where it was based for 9½ years. It ended its days at Lancaster on 20th October 1962, after a short period working the passenger and van trains to Leeds and achieved a total of 1,310,948 miles.

C. R. L. Coles

Seven months before it was attached to one of the straight high-sided 3,500 gallon tenders, of which there were ten and originally fitted to 'Jubilees', No. 45505 was named *The Royal Army Ordnance Corps* in 1947, although the name *Wemyss Bay* had been selected in 1943 but never carried. It was another member of the class to finish its days working the Leeds–Lancaster services, from Lancaster shed from where it was withdrawn on 2nd June 1962, having covered 1,377,946 miles in 30 years service. In September 1959 it is seen passing Tring with a down Manchester express having climbed steadily for almost the entire 31 miles from Euston.

C. R. L. Coles

An unidentified 'Patriot' roars past Cheddington on the long rising gradient to Tring with an up Liverpool boat train on a crisp day in 1959.

M. Welch

This heavy 16-coach train will have kept the fireman busy on an up Wolverhampton–Euston express. At the head of this train is No. 45546 *Fleetwood*, not looking in the best of condition, as it approaches Kilsby Tunnel with the radio masts visible in the background on 26th May 1953. It was allocated to Willesden for six years between November 1950 and November 1956. It had a wide sphere of operation during its 28 years service, possibly being the only unrebuilt example to be allocated to Kingmoor, for five months during 1934 for working the expresses over the Settle and Carlisle line to Leeds. It then moved to Holbeck for three months, before transferring to the Western Division. Final allocation was to Warrington on 23rd April 1960, from where it was withdrawn on 9th June 1962, a bad day for the unrebuilt locomotives as seven were withdrawn. It managed to cover 1,212,897 miles which was the next to lowest for the class.

J. P. Wilson

1953 appears to have been a bad year for clean unrebuilt 'Patriots' at Crewe North. No. 45513 emerges from the 1 mile 666 yards long Kilsby Tunnel after its climb away from Rugby on 26th May 1953 with an up express from Barrow. The locomotive was allocated the name *Sir W. A. Stanier* in 1943 which it never carried, and which one has to admit looked much more in place on the side of 'Princess Coronation' Pacific No. 46256. It was one of four members of the class to be withdrawn on 15th September 1962, when it was at Edge Hill.

J. P. Wilson

It was obviously a hot and sunny day on 20th June 1959 judging by the lack of exhaust from No. 45511 *Isle of Man* as it pulls away from Rugby on an up Manchester–Euston express, showing the interesting trackwork south of the station with the Northampton lines diverging to the right. This locomotive was at Willesden for just over eight years during the 1950s, but was allocated to a wide variety of depots, which involved no less than 22 transfers during its 29 years of service and 1,290,459 miles. The most interesting allocation was to Barrow Road, Bristol for six months between December 1934 and April 1935, and it was 23 years before another member of the class was transferred to this depot.

T. Boustead

No. 45531 *Sir Frederick Harrison* passes Rugby No. 1 signal box at the head of what was most likely an up express from Liverpool Lime Street to Euston. Although the picture is undated, it was taken during its lengthy allocation of over eleven years to Edge Hill, and as it is carrying the original BR tender emblem it was most likely taken in the early 1950s. After moving from Edge Hill, it finished its working days on mundane duties at Springs Branch, Wigan.

J. B. C. McCann

No. 45543 *Home Guard* passes non stop through Stafford at the head of a down express. The picture shows the station before it was rebuilt.

M. Welch

Another picture which shows part of the original station at Stafford as No. 45546 *Fleetwood* passes with an up relief.

M. Welch

No. 45515 *Caernarvon* makes a fine sight at the head of a 13-coach Llandudno–Euston express, as the tender overflows on Whitmore Troughs, about ten miles south of Crewe on 9th July 1955, which was during its 10½-year allocation to Edge Hill, between November 1949 and April 1960. After that its last transfer was to Newton Heath where it remained working secondary duties until withdrawn on 9th June 1962, having accumulated 1,355,294 miles. It also had a spell of three months at Holbeck in 1935, and later in that year moved to Shrewsbury for just one month. It was allocated one of the ten high-sided 3,500 gallon Fowler tenders for one month in 1957, from January to February, and again in August to a different one until March 1958. It had eight tender changes during its 30 years of service.

T. Lewis/Norman Preedy Collection

No. 45504 *Royal Signals* passes Madeley near the top of the long climb away from Crewe on an up fast express. It is showing a 5A Crewe North shedplate which means the picture was probably taken in the early 1950s as it was at that depot from October 1947 to January 1955. In November 1958 it was one of the three to be sent to Barrow Road, Bristol, from where it was withdrawn on 17th March 1962 with 1,274,026 miles covered in 30 years.

T. Lewis

The 8A shedplate indicates that No. 45534 *E. Tootal Broadhurst* was allocated to Edge Hill when this picture was taken as it left Crewe with an up express on 25th April 1959 with 158 miles to go before reaching Euston. This was in fact towards the end of its eight-year allocation to the depot which came to an end on 7th November 1959. It then moved briefly to Llandudno Junction before Crewe, Willesden, Llandudno Junction again and finally to Crewe North on 22nd June 1963 where it remained until withdrawn on 9th May 1964. It was next to the last to be rebuilt in December 1948, No. 45522 being the last. It managed a total of 1,685,322 miles in 31 years.

T. Boustead

In the Midlands

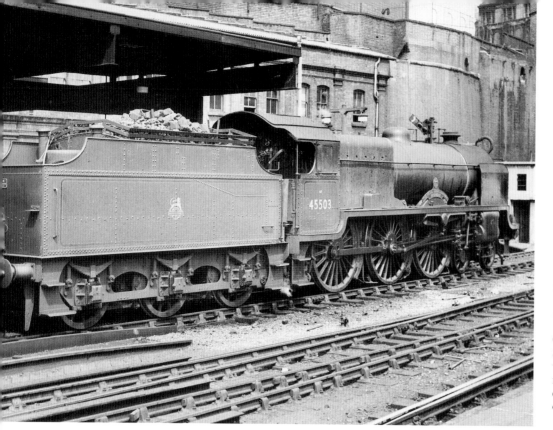

No. 45503 *The Royal Leicestershire Regiment* moved 21 times during its 29-years of service. Unfortunately the photograph is undated but it was most likely taken in the early 1950s when the locomotive was at Crewe North. The picture shows it ready to leave Birmingham New Street on an up train. It is remembered by the authors for when it took over from the preserved Midland Compound No. 1000 at Carnforth, on a Railway Correspondence & Travel Society Special to Ravenglass and gave what must have been one of the most lacklustre performances ever by a main line locomotive on one of their specials.

M. Welch

One of the first two 'Patriots' to be 'rebuilt' from 'Claughtons', No. 45501 *St Dunstan's* approaches Wellington on a humble stopping train from Shrewsbury to Stafford on 6th August 1956. A Longsight engine at the time of this photograph, it finished its days at Upperby on 26th August 1961 like many members of the class. It was reallocated 23 times during its 31 years of service during which it covered 1,266,776 miles. The depots at which it was allocated included Kentish Town, Holbeck, Patricroft, Carnforth, Mold Junction and Warrington, besides the other usual places for the class.

Brian Morrison

After rebuilding in November 1948 No. 45545 *Planet* was allocated to Bushbury for six months before being transferred to Camden on 28th May 1949, where it remained until 15th September 1956. Leaking badly, but nevertheless looking very handsome without smoke deflectors, and in the lined black livery with 'British Railways' lettering on the tender, it is shown storming out of Rugby on an up van train, possibly in 1949 or 1950.

J. B. C. McCann

A very fine action picture of No. 45529 *Stephenson* storming past Hillmorton on the climb south from Rugby on an up Wolverhampton–Euston express on 3rd August 1957 as the fireman leans out of the cab to check the injectors were working correctly. Allocated to Crewe North depot at the time of the photograph it moved twelve times between Crewe, Camden and Bushbury during the period to 1958, it ultimately ended its days along with some 'Royal Scots' at the former Great Central depot at Annesley from where it was withdrawn on 22nd February 1964, having covered 1,543,356 miles. During a short period around 1960 whilst at Willesden, the locomotive was stored at Devons Road for two months, before being returned to traffic.

J. P. Wilson

Looking in immaculate external condition No. 45534 *E. Tootal Broadhurst* is seen slowing for its Tamworth stop on an up express on 5th March 1960, whilst it was allocated to Llandudno Junction. It had probably just had a visit to Crewe Works, possibly for its last overhaul.

T. Boustead

A few unrebuilt members of the class finished up being allocated to Nuneaton for their final days. One of them was No. 45541 *Duke of Sutherland* which is shown here at Tamworth Low Level whilst it was allocated to Rugby from November 1959 to December 1960. It would appear that Nuneaton depot had very little work for their 'Patriots' as most photographs taken whilst they were at the shed show them on mundane freight or van train duties. No. 45541 was withdrawn on 9th June 1962 having covered 1,323,237 miles.

Norman Preedy

On 25th July 1959 No. 45534 *E. Tootal Broadhurst* heads the up 'Manxman' near Polesworth, between Tamworth and Nuneaton.

T. Boustead

A superb photograph of the only unrebuilt 'Patriot' to be allocated to Derby after Nationalisation. No. 45509 was named *The Derbyshire Yeomanry* whilst allocated to that depot in November 1951. It had been to the depot on 20th October 1951, but the allocation became permanent on 10th November and it remained there until 30th August 1958. It was generally very well looked after by the shed and could be seen working expresses to St Pancras, Bristol and north of Derby. It is shown leaving Nottingham, near London Road Junction, with an up Sunday Derby–St Pancras express on 22nd March 1953. It moved to Newton Heath on 30th August 1958 where it performed a variety of duties until being withdrawn on 12th August 1961 having accumulated 1,249,852 miles. The locomotive is recorded as being the only member of the class to have been damaged by enemy action during the war.

J. P. Wilson

Crewe–Carlisle

The second member of the class to be rebuilt, No. 45521 *Rhyl,* in October 1946, is shown weaving its way through the complex lay-out that used to exist at the north end of Crewe station. The picture was taken from the famous foot-bridge at this end of the station which spanned all the platforms and led to Crewe North shed. The picture is undated, but as the locomotive has the second style of emblem on the tender it must have been in the early 1960s. No. 45521 spent most of its time allocated to Edge Hill after it was rebuilt.

M. Welch

Two weeks following its allocation to Edge Hill, No. 45547 is seen approaching Hartford, just south of Weaver Junction where it will take the Liverpool line with the 2.15pm Euston–Liverpool on 24th June 1961. At this late stage in its career it is probable that it had taken the train over at Crewe. The 25kV overhead electrification was not energised at this time.

John Whiteley

Another picture taken at Hartford on 24th June 1961 shows Upperby-based No. 45512 *Bunsen* heading south on the 10.15am Edinburgh Princess Street–Birmingham New Street. It attained the highest mileage for any member of the class of 1,769,977, many of these being covered whilst allocated to Upperby between 28th May 1949 until withdrawal on 27th March 1965.

John Whiteley

By the early 1960s, when this picture was taken, most of the West Coast passenger duties were in the hands of diesels, so the rebuilt members of the class were regularly employed on freights, particularly between Crewe and Carlisle. No. 45530 *Sir Frank Ree*, running without nameplates, makes a fine sight as it climbs out of Warrington towards the Manchester Ship Canal Bridge near Acton Grange with an up freight for Crewe. It was the last of the class to be withdrawn in December 1965 with an estimated 1,740,019 miles.

J. R. Carter

No. 45527 *Southport* shuts off steam as it enters Warrington Bank Quay station with a northbound express on 28th August 1964. Close examination shows that the yellow stripe is painted on the cabside banning it from working south of Crewe. By this date, time was running out for this locomotive as it was withdrawn four months later. Rebuilt in September 1948, it was allocated to Edge Hill, in fact from December 1933 to March 1961 in both unrebuilt and rebuilt condition. Its days finished at Kingmoor on 5th December 1964, having covered 1,699,445 miles.

J. R. Carter

Allocated to Saltley depot at the time, No. 45540 *Sir Robert Turnbull* is seen in excellent lighting heading an up fish train from Fleetwood between Wigan North Western and Springs Branch depot. After its days on passenger work on the West Coast Main Line, it was allocated to depots on the Midland lines such as Trafford Park, Saltley, and Derby, before moving back to Upperby from where it was withdrawn on 6th April 1963 with an estimated 1,496,821 miles covered.

J. R. Carter

Upperby-allocated No. 45512 *Bunsen* enters Preston on a relief Crewe–Glasgow express on 26th March 1964. Note the array of fine gantries, which abounded at Preston. The locomotive still had another year to run before its withdrawal. It achieved the highest mileage of any member of the class.

M. Welch

No. 45548 *Lytham St. Annes* approaches Hest Bank, just north of Lancaster with a down freight on 22nd August 1954; the line diverging to the right is to Morecambe. It was allocated to Crewe North between January 1954 and November 1959 but finished its days in the Rugby division, allocated to Nuneaton from where it was withdrawn on 9th June 1962. It was one of the six members of the class to remain attached to the same tender (No. 4555) all the time.

R. J. Leslie

In terrible external condition No. 45535 *Sir Herbert Walker K.C.B.* rounds the curve towards Low Gill on a down Liverpool–Edinburgh express on 18th August 1962, having just passed Grayrigg Summit and is taking a breather before the climb from Tebay to Shap Summit. It was at Edge Hill at the time but moved to Kingmoor depot later in the year and remained in traffic until 26th October 1963 having covered an estimated 1,736,849 miles.

Gavin Morrison

One of the two prototype rebuilds carried out at Derby in 1930, was No. 45501 *St Dunstan's,* formerly No. 5902. The most readily identifiable parts of the original locomotive were the large wheel centres and radial bogie. It was allocated to Upperby at the time this picture was taken on 23rd May 1961, from where it was withdrawn on 26th August 1961. It is seen approaching Tebay in the Lune Gorge, with a northbound freight just before being faced with predominantly 1 in 75 climb to Shap Summit. It was reallocated no less than 23 times in its 27 years of service to a wide variety of depots such as Kentish Town, Holbeck and Mold Junction.

John Whiteley

No. 45524 *Blackpool* appears to be taking a run at Shap Bank as it storms through Tebay station without stopping for a banker. It was at Upperby depot at the time of this picture, 5th July 1960, shortly before moving to Warrington and finally Edge Hill from where it was withdrawn on 15th September 1962 with 1,290,093 miles covered. The locomotive depot at Tebay, which provided the Shap bankers, was situated behind the wall on the platform.

T. Boustead

After its seven-year period at Derby working the Midland lines, No. 45509 *The Derbyshire Yeomanry* was transferred to Newton Heath on 30th August 1958, where it worked out its days until withdrawal on 12th August 1961. Here it is seen approaching Scout Green on a CTAC Scottish Tours express on 9th July 1960, digging in on the 1 in 75 gradient to Shap Summit but showing little by way of exhaust on this warm summer day.

T. Boustead

On 27th July 1957 No. 45507 *Royal Tank Corps*, with the driver looking very relaxed, passes Scout Green intermediate signal box on its way up Shap Bank with a helping hand from a 2-6-4T at the rear. It was a Crewe North engine at the time before it went to Upperby, and finally to Lancaster where it worked out its days on the Midland line to Leeds until withdrawal on 20th October 1962.

R. J. Leslie

No. 45526 *Morecambe and Heysham* is about three quarters of the way up Shap Bank at Shap Wells at the head of train 1S71. It was at Upperby from 10th June 1950 until withdrawn on 24th October 1964, having been rebuilt in February 1947. It travelled 1,665,005 miles during its 31 years of service and was only transferred eight times. It had a spell at Holbeck depot on loan in 1947 after rebuilding for working alongside the rebuilt 'Royal Scots' on the Settle–Carlisle route.

M. Welch

The date of this photograph is unknown, but it must have been taken towards the end of its career as No. 45527 *Southport* has a yellow stripe on its cabside, banning it from working under the wires south of Crewe. It is shown about to enter the cutting near the top of Shap Bank faced with about 31 miles of predominantly down-hill running to Carlisle.

M. Welch

On Sunday, 12th July 1964 the driver of rebuilt No. 45512 *Bunsen* had obviously decided he didn't fancy tackling Grayrigg and Shap on his own with the 14-coach 9.30am Manchester–Glasgow–Edinburgh express, so 2-6-4T No. 42449 had been attached at Oxenholme as Tebay shed was closed. It certainly seems to be working hard with the summit in sight as it enters the cutting near the top of the 1 in 75 gradient.

John Whiteley

No. 45507 *Royal Tank Corps* restarts from a signal check at Shap Summit with an up express on 9th July 1960. The 12B shedplate indicates it was allocated to Upperby at the time.

T. Boustead

Another picture of the same train as seen in the previous picture showing No. 45507 slowing for a signal check at Shap Summit on 9th July 1960, having completed its almost unbroken 31 mile climb from Carlisle.

T. Boustead

On Easter Monday, 30th March 1964 an up relief was run for the 'Royal Scot' headed by Carlisle Upperby's No. 45512 *Bunsen*. It is seen passing the signal box at Thrimby Grange on the 1 in 125 southbound climb to Shap Summit.

John Whiteley

No. 45531 *Sir Frederick Harrison* passes Eamont Bridge Junction, shortly after passing Penrith, with a southbound milk train.

R. J. Leslie

Another picture of 1M23, as shown opposite with No. 45512 storming through the woods near Thrimby Grange towards Shap Summit on 30th March 1964. Neither photographer was aware of the other's presence on this rather gloomy Easter Monday.

R. J. Leslie

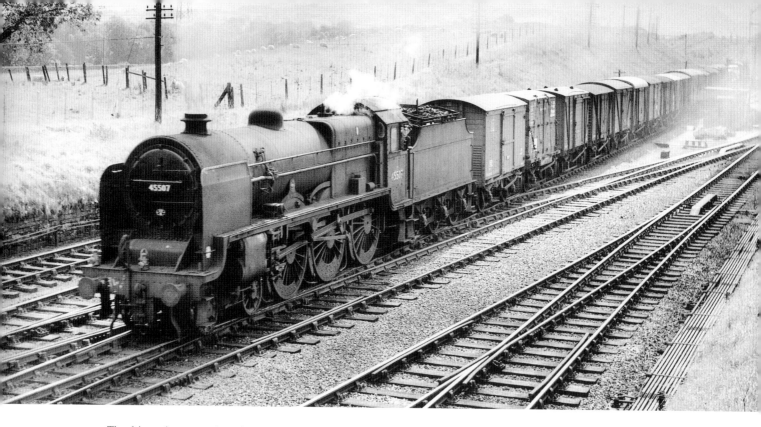

The driver gives a passing glance at the photographer as he was no doubt keeping his hand on the brake of No. 45507 *Royal Tank Corps* heading a down freight on the approach to Penrith on 26th August 1961. The line diverging to the right is the former Cockermouth, Keswick & Penrith line to Keswick. The locomotive is featured frequently in this section, no doubt due to its allocation to Upperby and Preston between 1958 and 1962, before its final transfer to Lancaster.

R. J. Leslie

Looking as if it had recently been to Crewe Works for overhaul, No. 45506 *The Royal Pioneer Corps,* heads south past Penrith with an up freight on 31st July 1958. It was an Upperby engine from January 1955 until 15th November 1958, when it moved with Nos 45504 and 45519 to Bristol Barrow Road to work cross country trains like the 'Devonian'. It remained there until withdrawn on 17th March 1962.

R. J. Leslie

The 7.11pm stopping train from Carlisle to Warrington used to enjoy a wide variety of motive power in the early 1960s and on 24th August 1961 No. 45547 was in charge, and is seen between Southwaite and Calthwaite heading south on the rising gradient from Carlisle. It had just been transferred to Edge Hill two months previously, where it ended its career on 15th September 1962.

R. J. Leslie

No. 45531 *Sir Frederick Harrison* managed to put in some useful main line passenger work during its allocation to Springs Branch depot to where it was sent on 19th October 1963. It is shown working an up troop train in fine style past Wreay on 23rd May 1964, about five miles south of Carlisle and still with a lot of hard work in front of it before reaching Shap Summit.

R. J. Leslie

No. 45549 was allocated the name *R.A.M.C.* in 1943, but this was never carried. There was a good covering of snow at Wreay on 13th February 1955, as it coasts down the 1 in 131 at the head of a Manchester–Glasgow express. It had an 8½-year allocation to Upperby between April 1950 and November 1958, and only had nine reallocations during its 28-year career. It finished its days at Warrington on 16th June 1962, its total mileage of 1,181,764 being the lowest for class by a margin of 31,000 miles. It was also one of the members of the class to remain attached to the same tender during its working days. Of special interest, No. 5549 was supposed to be allocated to Preston when new but apparently while it was heading north from Crewe it was instructed to be sent on to Polmadie where it is shown remaining until January 1941. It and No. 5550 appear to be the only members of the class to have been allocated at any time to Scotland. No. 5550 is shown as staying from new until December 1940, and it is interesting to speculate whether any picture exists of them at Polmadie at this time.

R. J. Leslie

No. 45512 *Bunsen* was allocated to Upperby for nearly 16 years, which was the longest period for any member of the class to remain at one depot, although No. 45526 stayed almost the same length of time at Bushbury. It is shown working hard past Brisco, shortly after leaving Carlisle with a 13-coach Glasgow–Manchester express on 14th May 1961.

R. J. Leslie

In poor external condition No. 45537 *Private E. Sykes V.C.* bursts from beneath the roof of Carlisle station with an Edinburgh–Manchester express on 3rd August 1953. Like many other members of the class it was allocated to Upperby depot at this time. By comparison with most other members it had very few transfers, only six during its 29-year career, which came to an end on 9th June 1962 when allocated to Nuneaton depot, with a total mileage of 1,304,901.

R. J. Leslie

It is hardly surprising that No. 45512 *Bunsen* appears much more frequently in these pages than other members of the class as it achieved the highest mileage with a total of 1,769,977. Many of these would have been during its 16 years at Upperby depot. Rebuilt in July 1948, it finished its days at Upperby on 27th March 1965. It is shown in this picture, having just arrived at Carlisle at the head of a down parcels train on 29th March 1964.

John Whiteley

North of England and North Wales

A group of enthusiasts at Leeds City observe the arrival of No. 45507 *Royal Tank Corps* on a train from Morecambe and Carnforth on 31st March 1962, just one month after it had been transferred to Lancaster to work these trains. Several of the class ended their days on these workings, No. 45507 finally being withdrawn on 20th October 1962.

John Whiteley

After turning on the triangle at Whitehall outside Leeds City, and visiting Holbeck depot for servicing No. 45507 *Royal Tank Corps* is ready to leave Leeds City at approximately 5.30pm with an evening return working back to Carnforth and Morecambe on Sunday 1st April 1962. The external condition of the locomotive was typical of the class allocated to Lancaster at the time.

John Whiteley

No. 45513 was an unnamed member of the class, but in 1943 it was allocated the name *Sir W. A. Stanier,* but it was never attached and would hardly have been appropriate. In typical condition for the time, it is seen leaving Leeds, near Wortley Junction, on 5th May 1961 heading the 1.54pm to Carnforth, where it was allocated at the time. Local Ivatt 2-6-0 No. 43044 waits to leave the gas works sidings. No 45513 was transferred to Edge Hill on 9th September 1961 from where it was withdrawn on 15th September 1962. It recorded the highest mileage for an unrebuilt member of the class, 1,462,043 miles, only 45,000 less than the lowest for a rebuilt locomotive.

Gavin Morrison

Another view of No. 45513 taken at the same location and working the same train as the previous picture, but on this occasion one month later. This photograph was taken from the long since demolished Wortley Junction signal box. The picture highlights the coal rails on the tender, No. 4490, and shows the breather pipe.

Gavin Morrison

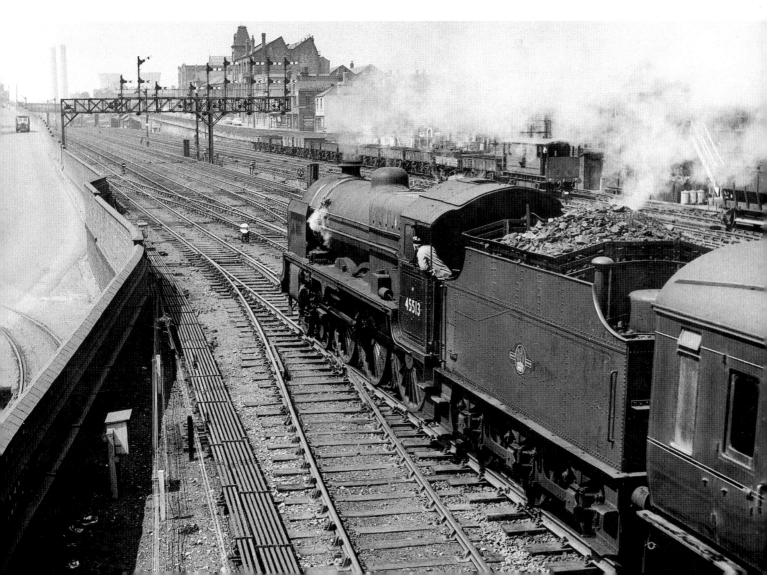

No. 45518 *Bradshaw* blows off as it slows for the sharp curve at Shipley, having just passed Guiseley Junction. The seven coach train from Leeds to Morecambe is in sharp contrast to today's two-coach 'Pacer' unit, and as can be seen from the lamp code on the smokebox, it was designated a stopping train. Lancaster based, and in the usual external condition, the locomotive was working out its last days on these trains, finally being withdrawn on 20th October 1962 with 1,373,516 miles covered during its career.

Gavin Morrison

No. 45522 *Prestatyn* was the last member of the class to be rebuilt, in February 1949. It was at Crewe North when it returned to traffic with short periods at Bushbury and Longsight before settling at Camden for over nine years until ousted by diesels, when it went to Kentish Town on 28th November 1959 and worked the Midland main line expresses. It is shown on one of these duties leaving Leeds City on 28th August 1961 with the 12.35pm to St Pancras. It was again rendered surplus by the 'Peak' diesels, and had a short spell at Newton Heath before its final move on 22nd June 1963 to Longsight. Its career came to an end at this depot on 19th September 1964 with a total mileage of 1,708,492.

Gavin Morrison

The Trans-Pennine services from Newcastle to Liverpool went over to diesel traction at the beginning of 1961, but during the summer timetable a relief train was run in front of the morning Newcastle–Liverpool from Leeds to Manchester departing at 12.35pm and was generally worked by an Upperby locomotive. The rebuilt 'Patriots', and occasionally an unrebuilt locomotive, usually worked this train, which travelled via the 'New Line' between Heaton Lodge, Mirfield and Farnley Junction, Leeds. On 29th August 1961 No. 45526 *Morecambe and Heysham* was in charge, and is shown on the climb to Gildersome & Birstall, having just crossed over the Dewsbury route at Farnley.

Gavin Morrison

No. 45531 *Sir Frederick Harrison* was a familiar sight on the Liverpool–Newcastle Trans-Pennine expresses during the 1950s when it was allocated to Edge Hill depot between June 1950 and October 1963. It is shown here emerging from the gloom of the tunnel into the sunshine at Huddersfield, on one of its regular duties, the morning express to Newcastle, which reached Huddersfield around 10.30am. These services went over to diesel traction at the beginning of 1961. Having been rebuilt in December 1947, it was finally withdrawn on 30th October 1965.

Gavin Morrison

A superb view of No. 45545 *Planet* storming across Saddleworth Viaduct towards the summit of the climb over the Pennines at Diggle. On this day in January 1963 the locomotive was standby engine at Edge Hill, and had to replace a diesel at very short notice due to a frozen train heating boiler, the train being the morning Liverpool–Newcastle express. It was allocated to Upperby at the time, and was finally withdrawn on 30th May 1964.

J. R. Carter

An Everton–Leeds football special is shown approaching Diggle having travelled via the Micklehurst loop from Stalybridge, and has just emerged from Butterhouse Tunnel (329 yards long). This route closed to all traffic on 20th October 1966. The locomotive is No. 45531 *Sir Frederick Harrison* which, at the time of this picture, 25th January 1964, was allocated to Springs Branch. It was no stranger to the route having worked the Trans-Pennine express for ten years between 1950 and 1960. It was withdrawn on 30th October 1965.

Gavin Morrison

The picture is dated 1961, which probably indicates that No. 45535 *Sir Herbert Walker K.C.B.* was substituting for a diesel, as these workings went over to diesel haulage at the start of the year. The train is the 9am Liverpool–Newcastle express and is shown running into Manchester Exchange. It was a frequent performer on these workings whilst allocated to Edge Hill between 12 June 1954 and 3rd November 1962.

J. R. Carter

No. 45531 *Sir Frederick Harrison* has appeared frequently in this section, no doubt due to its allocation to Edge Hill for 13 years. Here, it is leaving Manchester Exchange on one of its regular duties, the 9am Liverpool Lime Street–Newcastle. Due to the train being overloaded a banking engine was being used to assist up the 1 in 49 gradient to Miles Platting. Again, the picture is dated 1961, which suggests it was probably standing in for a failed diesel. Manchester Exchange has now been demolished and all tracks removed. The Class 5 in the picture left, is No. 45352.

J. R. Carter

After spending its entire working days from 1935 allocated to West Coast Main Line depots, it was rather a surprise when, on 26th July 1958, No 45517 was loaned to Bank Hall depot and transferred there permanently on 8th November 1958. The locomotive became a regular performer on the 10.30am Liverpool Exchange–Newcastle which was the prestige train of the day on the Calder Valley route. Here, it is seen blowing off as it passes over the water troughs at Luddendenfoot before slowing for a stop at Sowerby Bridge. The locomotive was generally well kept externally by Bank Hall, along with its three 'Jubilees', *Mars, Dauntless* and *Glorious*. One of the authors was fortunate to have a footplate ride on No. 45517 one day from Rochdale to Sowerby Bridge, and the sound of the exhaust on the climb to Summit Tunnel will long be remembered, even if the ride was rather rough. It was withdrawn from Bank Hall on 9th June 1962.

Gavin Morrison

The section of track between Heaton Lodge Junction, Mirfield, and Thornhill was originally shared by the Lancashire & Yorkshire and London & North Western railways, and was always very busy. Bank Hall's No. 45517 has just passed Mirfield on 24th April 1961 on its regular working, as described in the previous caption.

John Whiteley

No. 45532 *Illustrious* was rebuilt in July 1948, and then spent most of its time at Camden depot working West Coast Main Line expresses until ousted by diesels, when it was transferred to Nottingham on 21st November 1959. It spent a short spell of ten months, between June 1961 and April 1962, allocated to Saltley where, as the picture shows, it was well cleaned. It is leaving Pontefract Baghill on 29th June 1961 working the 3.50pm Newcastle–Birmingham. Like many of the rebuilt examples it finished its days allocated to Carlisle, in this case Upperby on 1 February 1964 with 1,718,594 miles credited to it.

P. Cookson

A powerful study of No. 45504 *Royal Signals* taken in August 1960 which was during the period when it, as well as Nos 45506 and 45519, was allocated to Bristol Barrow Road to assist the local allocation of 'Jubilees' working the cross country expresses to Birmingham, Leeds and York. It approaches Pontefract Baghill working the 12.48pm York–Bristol, which was one of their regular diagrams. All three were withdrawn on 17th June 1962.

P. Cookson

Post-war pictures of unrebuilt 'Patriots' working over the Settle and Carlisle line are very rare, but on 28th December 1957 No. 45502 *Royal Naval Division* was captured on film working a Leeds–Glasgow relief as it drifted down the 1 in 132 gradient at Cotehill. It was allocated to Carlisle Upperby at the time, being at this depot on four separate occasions during its career. It is interesting to note that although it was the first of the class to be withdrawn on 3rd September 1960, it achieved the second highest mileage of any of the unrebuilt locomotives, with a total of 1,388,595 miles, only exceeded by No. 45513. This was 206,837 miles more than that recorded by No. 45549 which had the lowest total, in spite of the fact that it remained in traffic for 21 months longer.

R. J. Leslie

In unrebuilt condition and before being named *Holyhead* in 1938, No. 5514 is shown working an express at Bell Busk, possibly in July 1935, no doubt en route to Carlisle. Records show it was allocated to Aston depot at the time. It was a widely travelled locomotive with 19 transfers in its almost 28 years of service, depots such as Shrewsbury, Aston, Holyhead, Bushbury and Derby being amongst them. It was the third to be rebuilt in March 1947 when it was at Edge Hill, and its career came to an end on 27th May 1961. It was also the first rebuilt 'Patriot' to be withdrawn by a margin of nearly two years, and only managed to exceed by 4,500 miles, the highest total for an unrebuilt member, with 1,507,446 miles.

W. H. Foster

A front end comparison between a rebuilt 'Royal Scot' and a rebuilt 'Patriot', showing detail differences in the two buffer-beams. The 'Scot' is No. 46163 *Civil Service Rifleman* which is on the centre road at Bangor heading a fast freight from Holyhead, whilst No. 45527 *Southport* has paused at the station at the head of a Holyhead–Euston train. Both locomotives were allocated to Holyhead (6J) at the time. The picture is dated 1963 but it must have been taken before 22nd June 1963, because No. 45527 was transferred to Willesden on that date. Its days finished on 5th December 1964 and the 'Royal Scot' was also withdrawn in 1964.

J. R. Carter

Against the picturesque background of Colwyn Bay, No. 45506 *The Royal Pioneer Corps* is shown leaving on 1st September 1953 when it was allocated to Crewe North. The locomotives were frequent visitors to the North Wales line, and both rebuilt and unrebuilt examples were allocated to Holyhead and Llandudno Junction, usually for short periods. This locomotive was one of three transferred to Bristol Barrow Road on 15th November 1958, where it finished its career on 17th March 1962.

R. E. Vincent

Standing under the superb overall roof at Manchester Exchange at Platform No. 2, sadly now but a memory, No. 45545 *Planet* is ready to leave on a local stopping train, the 10.50am to Wigan North Western via Tyldesley on 4th May 1963. Rebuilt in November 1948, it had just over a year of service left before being withdrawn from Carlisle.

J. R. Carter

When compiling books on particular classes of locomotives it is amazing how frequently pictures of certain ones crop up whilst others are very hard to find. No. 45518 *Bradshaw* perhaps has more than its fair share of coverage in these pages and here it is shown passing under Red Street signal gantry, Manchester, with empty stock off a West of England train, diverted to Ordsall Lane during the rebuilding of London Road station, now named Piccadilly. The picture was taken in the early 1960s when the 21D shedplate shows it was allocated to Aston. It finished its days at Lancaster depot on 21st October 1962.

J. R. Carter

No. 45512 *Bunsen* is surrounded by freight stock at Ordsall Lane goods sidings in Manchester on 27th February 1964, about a year before its withdrawal.

J. R. Carter

The station of Tyldesley closed on 5th May 1969, and the old LNW line has long since been consigned to the history books. No. 45531 *Sir Frederick Harrison*, another locomotive to feature frequently in the photographs in this book, is seen entering the station on a very mundane working, namely the 10.50am stopper to Wigan North Western from Manchester Exchange. Dated 1963 the photograph was taken during the locomotive's brief allocation to Springs Branch depot at the end of 1963 and early 1964.

J. R. Carter

Ready to leave Windermere with the up 'Lakes Express' is No. 45524 *Blackpool*. The date is 6th July 1960, when the locomotive was allocated to Carlisle Upperby, as indicated by the 12B shedplate. This portion of the train would join the other section from Keswick at Lancaster before proceeding to Euston.

T. Boustead

A long-time resident of Longsight depot after rebuilding, in fact for around twelve years except for a two months' stay at Northwich, No. 45530 *Sir Frank Ree* heads an up express past the London & North Western signal box at Cheadle Hulme in the late 1950s. This locomotive was rebuilt in October 1946, being the first of the class to receive this treatment, beating No. 45521 by two weeks. As it turned out it was the last of the class to be withdrawn, being condemned at Kingmoor depot on 1st January 1966.

T. Lewis

Double-headed workings

Looking very much cleaner than in several other pictures of it, unnamed No. 45510 makes an impressive sight as it leaves Manchester near Salford on the 9.50am train to Barrow in 1951, whilst allocated to Upperby. Blackpool-based Class 5 No. 44926 is providing assistance, no doubt as a way of returning it to its home depot.

J. R. Carter

It is hard to believe that main line locomotives in the early 1950s used to look as dirty as these two examples, but it was the norm rather than the exception. Although certain depots did manage to clean locomotives in this period they didn't seem to be on the West Coast Main Line. The up 'Welshman' is shown passing Rugeley on 30th June 1953, with more than adequate motive power in the form of No. 45545 *Planet,* and the unique rebuilt 'Royal Scot' No. 46170 *British Legion*, both locomotives being allocated to Camden depot at the time. *Planet* was rebuilt in 1948 and spent all of its time allocated to WCML depots, finally being withdrawn on 30th May 1964.

A. C. Cawston/John Whiteley Collection

Upperby-allocated No. 45544 receives a helping hand on the climb to Low Gill, by locally based Stanier 2-6-4T No. 42613. The heavy freight is shown just north of Oxenholme and the tank engine would most likely work through to Shap Summit. No. 45544 was attached to eight different tenders whilst covering 1,260,485 miles, ending its days allocated to Warrington and was withdrawn on 9th December 1961.

T. Boustead

Plenty of action in this picture as an unidentified Class 5 pilots No. 45548 *Lytham St. Annes* away from Rugby Midland in 1956. At that time No. 45548 was allocated to Crewe North, but did have a short spell at Rugby between April and December 1960 finishing its days at Nuneaton on 9th June 1962 having covered 1,243,530 miles.

J. B. C. McCann

Unfortunately we have few details of this photograph, other than it was obviously taken at Rugby showing a down train. The front locomotive is No. 45544 and is believed to be No. 45519 *Lady Godiva* at the rear. Pictures of pairs of unrebuilt 'Patriots' are very rare and if we have identified No. 45519 correctly, then it is likely that this photograph was taken before November 1958, when it was transferred to Bristol Barrow Road.

J. B. C. McCann

No. 45516 *The Bedfordshire and Hertfordshire Regiment* emerges from the shadows and into the winter sunshine, giving Bank Hall 'Jubilee', No. 45717 *Dauntless*, a helping hand with a Glasgow–Liverpool and Manchester express, on 31st December 1960. No. 45516's claim to fame occurred back in February 1950 when it was allocated to work a special troop train for the Regiment, from Southampton Docks along the London & South Western main line, when it was still in crimson lake livery. At the time this photograph was taken it was allocated to Warrington from where it was withdrawn in July 1961 having covered 1,330,644 miles.

R. J. Leslie

An impressive picture taken at Cheddington, of Willesden-allocated No. 45547 piloting a rebuilt 'Royal Scot' on a down express in 1959. No. 45547 had around 14 allocations during its career, covering 1,227,221 miles, all to sheds on the West Coast Main Line except for a short period at Llandudno Junction in 1961. It was withdrawn from Warrington depot on 15th September 1962.

M. Welch

Generous motive power for the down 'Midlander' as it passes Kenton headed by No. 45545 *Planet* and 'Jubilee' No. 45737 *Atlas* in June 1957. The 5A shed-plate indicates it was allocated to Crewe North, where it had been since the previous month and where it remained until being transferred for the last time on 10th June 1961 to Upperby. Withdrawal came on 30th May 1964 after an estimated 1,701,922 miles.

C. R. L. Coles

No. 45509 *The Derbyshire Yeomanry* was the only member of the class to be allocated to Derby for any length of time, in fact from November 1951 to August 1958. It was named *The Derbyshire Yeomanry* in 1951 and was used all over the Midland main lines and was generally well cleaned, but on 30th August 1958 it was transferred for the last time to Newton Heath where it remained until withdrawal on 12th August 1961. During this period it was occasionally seen on the east side of the Pennines around Leeds, and on Sunday 28th February 1960 it was rostered to work the famous Heaton–Red Bank empty vans train, which is shown leaving Leeds City, coupled to Llandudno Junction-based Class 5 No. 44865. This working was renowned for its variety of motive power combinations and on this day arrived at Leeds with Gateshead A4 No. 60016 *Silver King* piloting the Class 5, regrettably not captured on film by the photographer.

Gavin Morrison

Freight and parcels traffic

Photographed about a year to go before it finished its duties on the WCML, primarily working freights and whilst allocated to Carlisle Upperby, No. 45510 was transferred to Lancaster to finish its days working the Leeds passenger/parcels trains. One of the unnamed locomotives, it is seen drifting downhill towards Carlisle from Wreay with a freight for Upperby Yard. It had eight transfers in its working career, which finished on 9 June 1962. Picture dated 31st March 1961.

R. J. Leslie

No. 45537 *Private E. Sykes V.C.*, in poor external condition, is shown heading an up freight past Wreay. Compared with other unrebuilt members of the class it had few shed reallocations, only moving six times in its working career.

R. J. Leslie

Showing a Carlisle Upperby shedplate, No. 45505 *The Royal Army Ordnance Corps*, and attached to one of the ten Fowler high-sided tenders (No. 4569) which it had acquired on 2nd April 1960, is seen approaching Acton Grange with a heavy Carlisle–Crewe freight late in 1960.

J. R. Carter

No. 45526, named *Morecambe and Heysham* in 1937, and rebuilt in February 1947, leads a down express freight past Hest Bank on 24th August 1961.

P. Cookson

Whilst allocated to its final depot, Edge Hill, unnamed No. 45547 is rather off its usual haunts at Lenton South Junction, Nottingham, with a very mixed freight on 14th September 1961.

T. Boustead

A picture taken very near to the end of its career shows No. 45519 *Lady Godiva,* passing Tuffley on its way into Gloucester with a lengthy freight from Bristol to the Midlands. When it was withdrawn in March 1962 it had 1,366,224 miles to its credit. It was one of the six members of the class to run with the same tender throughout its career, oddly enough the other two Barrow Road locomotives, Nos 45504 and 45506, did the same.

Norman Preedy

A very fine study of unrebuilt No. 45506 *The Royal Pioneer Corps* taken when it was allocated to Crewe North between September 1952 and January 1955 as it left Rugby with an up van train. It was allocated to most of the main line depots on the West Coast Main Line until 15th November 1958 when surprisingly, it was allocated to Bristol Barrow Road, along with Nos 45504 and 45519 from where they were all withdrawn on 17th March 1962.

J. B. C. McCann

Only two months before its withdrawal, and in terrible external condition, No. 45510 works out its last days allocated to Lancaster on passenger and parcels duties to Leeds. It is working the afternoon vans to Morecambe past Wortley Junction, Leeds on 12th April 1962.

Gavin Morrison

Unrebuilt members of the class do not seem to have been captured on film very often north of the border, whilst rebuilt locomotives were common visitors. No. 45535 *Sir Herbert Walker K.C.B.,* rebuilt in September 1948, is seen passing Auchterarder, south of Perth with a van train towards the end of its career when it was allocated to Carlisle Kingmoor, between 3rd November 1962 and 26th October 1963. Kingmoor depot never had an allocation in the days when it was part of the Scottish Region as 68A, and only received some of the rebuilt examples at the end of their time, mainly to work secondary duties.

A. C. Cawston/John Whiteley Collection

A superb study of No. 45511 *Isle of Man* passing Penrith with an up freight with a full head of steam. The picture is greatly enhanced by the human interest by way of the permanent way gang. This was a fine location used by many famous photographers, but sadly is now something consigned to history. The picture was taken between April and September 1960, as the engine is displaying an 8B (Warrington) shed code. It was finally transferred to Upperby in September 1960 from where it was withdrawn the following February.

W. P. Connolly

A powerful picture of No. 45539 *E. C. Trench* heading a down fitted freight past Kenton, whilst allocated to Willesden depot in 1959. It was one of two of the class allocated to Newton Heath depot, the only other being No. 45515, which survived until 1962. It was also one of the four members of the class to be paired to a high-sided Fowler tender, which it received in May 1956, but lost the following January. No. 45539 is recorded as having covered 1,280,744 miles.

M. Welch

Pictures of the class working trains tender-first are not very common, but with its days on regular main line passenger duties well behind it by 31st August 1963, No. 45532 *Illustrious* is allocated a humble ballast train, and is shown passing Penrith. Rebuilt in 1948, it spent the majority of its time at Camden in this form until displaced by the English Electric Type 4 diesels, after which it had spells at Nottingham, Saltley and Derby between November 1959 and June 1962, before finishing its days at Upperby on 1st February 1964.

M. Welch

Unrebuilt No. 45510 appears frequently in this section, always in terrible external condition. On 1st April 1961 it makes a dramatic departure at Winwick Junction, north of Warrington, on a down freight, having allowed the 'Mid-Day Scot' to overtake. Allocated to Upperby at the time, it was transferred to Lancaster on 10th February 1962 and was eventually withdrawn on 9th June 1962.

Hugh Ballantyne

This photograph, taken during the early 1960s, shows rebuilt No. 45512 *Bunsen* heading north near Winwick Junction with a Crewe–Carlisle freight. After rebuilding in July 1948, it had a short spell allocated to Bushbury before being transferred to Upperby on 28th May 1949 where it remained for the next 16 years before withdrawal.

J. R. Carter

The light exhaust stands out well against an overcast sky, as No. 45526 *Morecambe and Heysham* heads north beyond the bridge carrying the West Coast Main Line over the Manchester Ship Canal, just south of Warrington Bank Quay. At the time of this 1963 view, No. 45526 was allocated to Upperby depot, where it remained for 14 years until withdrawn on 24th October 1964.

J. R. Carter

As No. 45512 *Bunsen* achieved the highest mileage for any member of the class, it is not surprising that it appears to have been well photographed. An unusual and impressive top view is shown here, taken at Ordsall Lane, Manchester, when it had been 'borrowed' for this freight working by Patricroft depot due to a shortage of the usual motive power. It was taken on 27th February 1964, just over a year before its withdrawal from Upperby depot.

J. R. Carter

Allocated to Warrington (8B) at the time of this photograph, 9th April 1960, No. 45518 *Bradshaw* is shown south of Wreay heading an up freight on the West Coast Main Line. Close observation reveals that this locomotive had the cabside numbers slightly higher than most members of the class. *Bradshaw* survived until 20th October 1962 working out its final days from Lancaster depot on trains to Leeds.

R. J. Leslie

The trio of long-time resident Upperby rebuilt examples, namely Nos 45512, 45526 and 45532, feature frequently in this section. This fine study of No. 45532 *Illustrious* shows it working a mundane coal train on the Tyldesley branch at Sandersons Sidings near Worsley during 1962. Another case of Patricroft depot being short of suitable motive power.

J. R. Carter

Looking unusually clean for an Upperby unrebuilt 'Patriot' in 1960, No. 45507 *Royal Tank Corps* makes a fine sight as it climbs Shap Bank, past Shap Wells with a Fowler 2-6-4T assisting at the rear. No. 45507 was reallocated 17 times during its career, and was another member of the class which worked out its days at Lancaster, being withdrawn on 20th October 1962.

Gavin Morrison

In dramatic lighting conditions No. 45531 *Sir Frederick Harrison* climbs Shap Bank near Scout Green on a down freight, with assistance at the rear. The date was 27th August 1964 when it was allocated to Carlisle Kingmoor until withdrawal on 30th October 1965. The diagonal yellow stripes can just be seen on the cab side, indicating the locomotive was banned from working under the wires south of Crewe.

M. Welch

On Shed

An impressive view of No. 5507 *Royal Tank Corps* on Camden depot, with a 3A shedplate indicating it was allocated to Bescot depot at the time. It must have presented a superb sight in its red LMS livery. It received its name during 1937, the year in which this photograph was taken. 'Royal Scot' No. 6108 *Seaforth Highlander* can be seen in the background fitted with a Stanier tender and both locomotives are being prepared for their next turns of duty from Euston.

Brian Morrison

The coal is piled very high on the tender of No. 45503 *The Royal Leicestershire Regiment* as it waits for its next working, in the dismal surroundings of what was then its home base of Crewe North, on 20th August 1955.

Brian Morrison

This view shows two of Carlisle Upperby depot's long time resident rebuilt 'Patriots', plus rebuilt 'Royal Scot' No. 46127 *Old Contemptibles* (then withdrawn) on the right. On the left is No. 45526 *Morecambe and Heysham* with No. 45512 *Bunsen* alongside, 6th April 1963.

Gavin Morrison

No. 45505 was named *The Royal Army Ordnance Corps* in 1947, and is seen at Edge Hill depot, Liverpool, with plenty of coal, when it was attached to one of the straight high-sided 3,500 gallon/7 tons coal capacity tenders, which it received on 2nd April 1960. These tenders, of which there were ten, were originally fitted to 'Jubilees' Nos 5607 to 5616, but in later years were attached to many classes including Fowler 4Fs and Stanier 8Fs. The locomotive was allocated to Longsight at the time this picture was taken late in 1960.

J. R. Carter

No. 45512 *Bunsen* is seen on the turntable at Newton Heath depot ready to work an express to the North from Manchester Victoria on 7th December 1963.

Gavin Morrison

No. 45504 *Royal Signals*, named in 1937, is shown under the coaling plant at Holbeck depot, Leeds, after working the 'Devonian' from Bristol on 3rd June 1959. The 82E shed plate indicates it was under the control of the Western Region and was allocated to Bristol Barrow Road depot. In addition to working cross county expresses from Bristol to Birmingham, Leeds and York, the three Bristol-based 'Patriots' were apparently also used on fitted freights to the North and even trips into South Wales on coal trains. No. 45504 was attached to the same tender, No. 4476, during the whole of its career.

Gavin Morrison

No. 45545, named *Planet* in 1948, awaits its next duty at the back of Holbeck depot on 5th April 1964. Considering the locomotive was withdrawn on 30th May, it was in remarkably good external condition. It was rebuilt in November 1948 and was allocated mainly to Crewe North and Camden in its rebuilt form, but finished its days at Upperby. This view shows its Stanier tender, No. 9773, to which it was attached permanently following rebuilding in 1948, and also the Stanier cab which was the main external distinguishing feature between the rebuilt 'Patriots' and the rebuilt 'Royal Scots'.

Gavin Morrison

The external condition of those members of the class which finished their working days at Lancaster was terrible, as can be seen in this picture of No. 45518 *Bradshaw* taken at Holbeck on 24th April 1962, six months before withdrawal on 20th October.

Gavin Morrison

The movement shown by the steam from the safety valves of No. 45501 *St Dunston's* suggests this was a very dull day and a long exposure and a tripod were necessary. Note the design of the nameplate, which was completely different from the rest of the class. No. 45501, originally LMS No. 5902, was the second of the two prototype rebuilds carried out at Derby in 1930, although as previously noted, very little of the original locomotives were used. The photograph was taken at Shrewsbury depot on 21st July when the locomotive was allocated to Longsight.
Brian Morrison

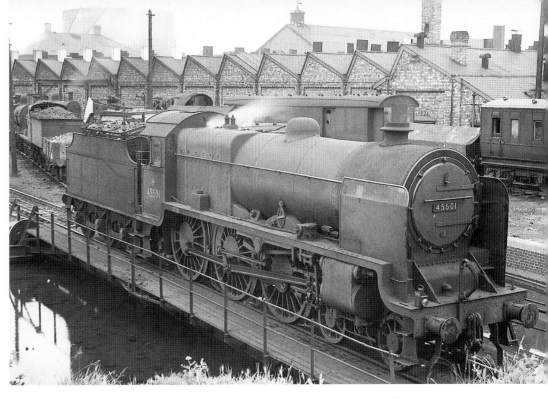

One of the ten members of the class never to carry a name was No. 45547 shown here at Willesden, its home depot at the time in 1960. It spent its entire working life allocated to West Coast Main Line depots except for brief spells at Newton Heath in 1934 and Llandudno Junction in 1961, finally ending its days at Edge Hill on 15th September 1962.
M. Welch

A fine picture of Patricroft depot where the photographer worked for several years, shows No. 45545 *Planet* ready to leave for its next duty in 1962.

J. R. Carter

It is likely that the photographer may have had some influence in setting up this interesting photograph comparing the slightly different front ends of the rebuilt 'Royal Scots' and 'Patriots', which was taken at Patricroft depot in 1963. No. 45534 *E. Tootal Broadhurst*, was allocated to Llandudno Junction at the time and had previously had another spell at the same depot in 1959, as well as being loaned to Holyhead in 1950. Otherwise, in its rebuilt form, it was at the main depots for working expresses on the West Coast Main Line. It was withdrawn in May 1964, whereas No. 46157 *The Royal Artilleryman,* only lasted until January 1964.

J. R. Carter